Introduction: Christians Need to Know about Islam

Only an ostrich can ignore Islam today.

The bastion of Islam stands in the sure knowledge of its immense political and economic power. In the United Nations the Muslim nations control a sizeable slice of the Third World vote. Their oil wealth gives them untold influence over other nations too: their carrot of vast sums of aid is balanced by the threatening stick of a possible rise in oil prices or perhaps a total oil boycott. Even nations like the United States and Canada sigh with relief when Sheikh Yamani gives a conciliatory smile, and we shudder down our economic spine whenever he frowns in displeasure at an unwise political statement by our leaders or at an offensive television film about the death of a princess. In days of recession and unemployment we all desperately need the goodwill of the oil-rich Muslim nations of the Middle East.

1 Islam's new power

No longer can we simply divide the world into the old power blocks of the Western world, the Communist countries and the so-called Third World. Today we have to take into account the powerful grouping of the Islamic nations. This fact is almost a truism, for the reality of the power of Islam and the influence of oil has forced itself into the consciousness of us all. Indeed it is hard to realise that this situation is quite new. Only a very few years ago the Muslim nations of the Middle East wallowed in backward poverty. The recent past already seems light years away.

Take Libya for example. Their oil only began to flow in 1961 and even then it took several years to build up to its present huge potential. Names like Tripoli and Tobruk used to feature as desert outposts. Rival armies fought over them in the Second World War, but otherwise they had little significance. However, by 1967 oil revenues had revolutionised this formerly insignificant kingdom. Under Italian colonial government Libyans were only permitted to attain education up to Grade Five: now university faculties have mushroomed in Tripoli and Benghazi. Urbanisation has begun to change the whole way of life. Population has grown by some 3.6 per cent a year until half the total population is under fifteen years of age. Political change followed with an army coup in 1969 and the emergence of the radical and ambitious Muslim Colonel Gaddafi. Since then it has been impossible to ignore Libya. The combination of fanatical Islam with oil wealth and confidently dynamic ambition has made Libya a force to be reckoned with. It may be that the majority of the country is still desert and that there are still only about three million Libyans, but today no one can snap their fingers at Libya with impunity.

What is true of Libya is at least equally true of Saudi Arabia and the Gulf States. Their power in politics and economics causes all other nations to woo them. Just a few years ago such names as Bahrain or Qatar were known only to the very rare person who enjoyed an interest in remote desert wildernesses. Today they are household names. Their rulers determine the state of our purses and cause us to exclaim every time we put gas into our cars.

None of us today dares ignore the revolutionary struggles in Iran. Their battles affect us. Conservative Islam wrestles with the westernising tendencies which almost inevitably accompany greater national wealth. We need to understand something about Islam if we are to appreciate what is happening there and what is the likely influence of their revolution on the rest of the Middle East. This was brought even closer to us by the American hostage situation and the media attention on Iran that accompanied it.

Likewise the battle between the Soviet forces of Marxism and the militant Muslim insurgents of Afghanistan has been well publicised. Again we need to know something about Islam if we are to understand why the different Afghan tribes cannot unite in this battle or how Afghanistan relates to her Muslim Pakistani and Iranian neighbours. The significance of this struggle will only be seen if we also know something of the fifty million Muslims within the borders of the Soviet Union herself.

Islam is never far away from our television news headlines – even if only in the reporting of the scandals of rigid enforcement of Muslim criminal law in Saudi Arabia, Libya or Pakistan.

2 Islam challenges Christianity

It is not only the political and economic significance of Islam which forces us to take it seriously and make real efforts to learn more about it. The political and economic power of Islam has given Muslims a new confidence also in the superiority of their religion.

In various parts of the world Islam and Christianity oppose each other in their mission activity. In many countries of Africa the people are dissatisfied with their traditional tribal faiths. They are searching for a new religion, preferably a major world faith. Islam and Christianity are the two obvious alternatives. They vie with one another in competition for the souls of men. Anyone living or working in Africa today must have a good grasp of the tenets of Islam.

In Asia too the Christian Church is sometimes locked in a fierce struggle for survival. Islamic lands like Pakistan and

Malaysia apply economic and social pressures, pushing Christians to convert to Islam. At times job promotion depends on being a Muslim. In other situations the authorities actually bribe local people to be circumcised as Muslims. The mass media feature Islamic teaching, mosque prayers and news items about Christians who have converted to Islam. The pressure is on. Christians need to know how to withstand the teachings of Islam and present the Christian message in ways that are relevant to a Muslim context.

Some of us may feel that Africa and Asia are a long way away. We may be tempted to feel therefore that Islam is irrelevant to us. But the facts reveal the folly of any such blinkered thoughts. In North America and most of the countries of western Europe there are today large numbers of Muslim students and immigrants. About 2 million Muslims live in the United States today. In addition, students from Muslim countries constitute the largest group of international students in North American colleges and universities. In some cases these Muslims are active in mission.

(a)   Muslims come to us

Until very recently Muslims were a rare curiosity in North America. Most of us never met them. But things have changed. Oil money gushed from Middle Eastern coffers to pay for large numbers of students and official visitors to our country.

A few years ago one of my children was travelling by train in the south of England. Boredom lulled him into dreamland. Then he opened his eyes and to his amazement saw a mosque flash by outside. Was it a dream? Was he back in Asia again? Just a few years ago we did not expect to see a mosque in Britain. But now in this generation oil money has financed the erection of many large and beautiful mosques in the cities of Europe and the United States.

The huge Islamic Center in Washington, D.C., is a symbol of Muslim unity and of the emergence of Islam as a major religious tradition in North America. New mosques are being built all the time in urban centers such as New York and Chicago, and these projects are frequently funded with oil money from the Middle East.

When visiting university Christian groups I am often asked how students can witness more effectively to Muslims. They have discovered that their usual forms of witness do not seem to communicate. Sadly they seem to know little about Islam; the speakers they invite to their meetings rarely relate Christian doctrine to Islamic beliefs. The students therefore have no idea how to share their Christian understanding of God, salvation or revelation with a Muslim. And when a Muslim student attacks them on the doctrine of the Trinity and denies that Jesus is the Son of God, they have little ability to defend their beliefs.

This failure to understand Islam relates equally to our churches. Ignorance of even the basics of Islam can be a major obstacle to effective Christian witness in many churches. One flourishing church I know of found that many of those who lived near the church were Pakistani Muslims. They longed to share the glories of life in Christ with them. And so they agreed to distribute a Gospel to every home. Sadly, they chose Mark's Gospel. This may be ideal for many non-Christians, but proves offensive to Muslims because of its opening verse: "The beginning of the Gospel of Jesus Christ, the Son of God" (Mark 1:1). Few Muslims will read on. They bridle at the thought of Jesus as God's Son, a doctrine which they strongly reject. The church would have been wiser to distribute Luke's Gospel which relates more closely to Muslim ideas about Jesus.

(b) We go to them
The air tickets are not all in one direction!

High unemployment in the United States and Canada contrasts vividly with the enormous wealth and unbounded opportunities for trade and work in the oil-rich Muslim nations. The enticements of huge salaries outweigh the snags of stifling heat and the severe limitations with regard to alcoholic drinks, entertainments and social life. People of all nations flock to Saudi Arabia, the U.A.E., Kuwait and other Islamic lands. There they come face to face with Islam.

I live in quite a small village. One might think that this book on Islam would be irrelevant to people there. We have no Muslims living there. But recently the school "lollipop lady" stopped me in the street. "What is Islam like in Libya?" she asked me. "My husband is an engineer and cannot find work." She then told me that he had been offered a job in Libya. She had heard stories of the segregation of women in Saudi Arabia and was anxious about going to a strongly Muslim country. I explained to her that the Muslims of Saudi Arabia follow a different and stricter sect of Islam. Yes, even in rural areas we need to know about Islam.

When North Americans travel to solidly Muslim countries they can react in two different ways. Some become decidedly anti-Muslim, but others are attracted. Let me give an example.

A Pentecostal pastor found himself in an Islamic country, but knew nothing about Islam. He had never before met a Muslim. The regular discipline of the five daily calls to prayer and the apparent piety of ordinary people made him question the power and validity of his own faith. He began to doubt the claims of Jesus Christ to be the unique way, truth and life (John 14:6). Might not Islam be a better and truer religion? This experience has shattered his ministry and changed his whole life. He needed a Christian with knowledge of Islam to stand alongside him at that crucial stage of his life. Many Christians today are having to face the reality of Islam and other faiths. This challenges all that they believe. We need to know enough to be able to help.

But our study of other religions will not only be in order to help others. We too shall face the same battles as that Pentecostal pastor. Muslims are stressing the priority of mission to other peoples. According to Salem Azzam, secretary general of the Islamic Council of Europe: "Islam is once again on the march." The first objective of the Islamic Council is "to assist, support and supplement the activities . . . of *da'wah* (mission)".

Both Christians and Muslims have become aware that mission can only achieve its purposes if built on a foundation of a true community of believers. As I have demonstrated in *Don't Just Stand There*, the Old Testament calling for Israel was that the gentiles should be attracted in to Zion by the life of God's people. This was fulfilled in Jesus Christ and then the Church was commanded to move out in evangelistic proclamation. Islamic *da'wah* also concentrates largely on strengthening the Muslim community, but it does not lose sight of the goal of converting non-Muslims.

The work of *da'wah* is fulfilled not only by direct preaching, tract distribution and personal persuasion, but also by the more subtle approach of cultural exhibitions and mass media presentations about Islamic art and culture.

Through living contact with Islam or other faiths, many Christians have quietly slipped into the belief that all religions can give their followers the knowledge of God and his salvation. So universalism creeps into our churches. It undermines the very foundations of Christian faith and mission. All of us need therefore to know what we believe and why we believe it. We need also to understand other peoples' faiths, including Islam. This book is written to try to help us as Christians to interact with Islam.

3   What does Islam believe?

As we proceed in this book, we shall note that Islam is not as clear-cut as it may at first appear. But the westerner's first impressions will probably confirm the Muslim's claim to a simple, uncomplicated faith. An apparently uncluttered theology works itself out in a seemingly rigid, puritanical way of life. A deeper knowledge of current movements in Islam may give the lie to it, but a superficial view of Islam reveals a male-dominated society with strict taboos on drink and tobacco.

What then does Islam believe? It may be helpful at this stage to give a brief and simple outline of the basics of Islam.

(a)   One God

The central plank in the Muslim faith is a strict monotheistic belief in one God. The Muslim creed states firmly that there is no God but Allah. All other deities are vain idols. Allah alone is God. He is the one sovereign creator of the world. He is supremely great and none can be compared or associated with him. He is so perfect that it is blasphemous to suggest that he could have a son.

(b)   Mohammed

Linked to the uniqueness of God in the Muslim creed is the affirmation that Mohammed is God's prophet. Mohammed makes no claims to deity. He is sent by God as a messenger to bring the message of God to men. He comes as God's signpost to show men the way.

There were many prophets before Mohammed (including Abraham and other Old Testament figures), but he is the final prophet. Other nations and peoples had their prophets, but Mohammed came as the messenger of God to the Arabs and then, through the Arabs, to the rest of the world.

(c) Heaven and hell

God's word through Mohammed clearly warns men of the dangers of hell and the beautiful possibility of heaven. Believers in the one God will probably be granted the bliss of heaven with all the pleasures thereof. Idolators are liable for the penalty of hell. Judgment according to the will of God is based fundamentally on a man's works.

(d) The Quran

God has sent a variety of Holy Books through several prophets even before the coming of Mohammed. The four main Books are the Law through the prophet Moses, the Psalms through the prophet David, the Gospel through the prophet Isa (Jesus) and then finally the Quran through the prophet Mohammed. Just as there will be no further prophets after Mohammed, so too the Quran brings this series of divine Books to its end.

The Quran was originally written on a tablet in Heaven by God himself. Mohammed played no part in forming the contents of the Quran. He merely acted as the channel through whom God sent down his revealed message to men. The Quran is therefore totally divine without any human influence or participation.

God's revelation comes through the ministry of angels. Belief in angels stands therefore as a basic tenet of Islam.

(e) The Five Pillars

The faith of Islam is demonstrated by submission to the will of God which is particularly seen in the five pillars of Islam.
(i) Faith   All Muslims must subscribe to the simple credal statement that there is no god but Allah and that Mohammed is his prophet. This creed will be recited frequently throughout life and finally to the angels of judgment in the grave.

(ii) Prayer   Five times each day the faithful are called to
the ritual prayers of Islam. On Fridays it is customary that
every Muslim should be in the mosque for at least one of
these five prayer times, but on other days Muslims may
fulfil their prayers wherever they happen to be. Strict
rituals are laid down on how to purify the place where one
prays, how to perform one's ritual washing and the exact
movements and words of the prayers themselves. The final
act of the prayers is prostration, when every Muslim sym-
bolically bends in submission to Allah with his forehead to
the ground.

(iii) The fast   Through the entire month of Ramadan each
year all Muslims must refrain from allowing anything to
pass the throat during the hours of daylight. Before dawn
and after sundown the Muslim may eat and drink to his
heart's content, but through the long hours of the day he
may neither eat nor drink. In a hot climate such self-
discipline is costly.

(iv) Alms   The law of Islam lays down detailed and strict
regulations about how much a Muslim must give in alms to
the poor. Mohammed himself was an orphan from a poor
family, so the care of the poor played a vital part in his
teaching. The almsgiving law exemplifies the reforming
role which the new religion of Islam played in the social
setting of Mecca and Medina. In the light of current debates
about accumulated wealth it is interesting to note that alms
were given according to a man's capital, not just his in-
come.

(v) Pilgrimage   Before the time of Mohammed it was
already customary in Arabia to make the pilgrimage to the
great black meteorite stone in Mecca. Under Islam this
ancient practice was given a new theological dress, but the
basics of the pilgrimage rite continued as before. Today it is
mandatory that every Muslim man should perform the
pilgrimage to Mecca at least once in his lifetime, unless

ill-health, extreme poverty or some other major problem prevents it.

This brief summary of the faith of Islam is of course fearfully shallow and unsatisfactory, but it may help the reader as we go deeper into Islam in the coming chapters.

Conclusion

In earlier years it was still possible to receive theological training without being introduced at all to Islam. Thus, when I studied at an evangelical theological college some twenty years ago, we were taught nothing at all about Islam. On beginning my career as a missionary among Muslims in South-East Asia I had never even read the Quran and knew nothing whatsoever about the Muslim faith. Today no training for ministry overseas could possibly be considered adequate without considerable teaching on this subject.

The need for a serious attempt to understand Islam is clear in our churches. It is encouraging to see courses on Islam being offered at institutions such as Gordon-Conwell Theological Seminary and the Fuller School of World Mission. Inter-Varsity's Student Missions Convention at Urbana (held every three years) also offers numerous seminars for students interested in Muslim evangelism.

Happily there have appeared a number of popular books on Christian witness among Muslims during these last few years. The church needs them. Regretfully I fear that many of them fail to adapt to the thought forms and feelings of the Muslim. I hope this book will introduce the reader to Islam as it really is. I shall give hints on how to witness to a Muslim, but I shall resist the temptation to give a simplistic how-to-do-it answer. It would be unrealistic to pretend that it is easy to engage in witness among Muslims. We are only scratching the surface.

1
Islam Faces the Outside World

For centuries Christians and Muslims have pursued their separate paths with minimal contact. Each has been largely ignorant of the other with the result that we face a major struggle today to educate our people to grapple with the challenges of a cosmopolitan world. But this was not always the case in earlier periods of history.

1 Historical contacts

(a) Early Islam

In the early centuries of Islam, after the death of Mohammed in 632 A.D., Muslims interacted very considerably with the outside world. Four great leaders known as the orthodox caliphs succeeded Mohammed. During their reigns, which lasted until 661 A.D., Islam confronted not only the surrounding Arab tribes, but also the great empires of Persia, Byzantium and Rome. Within a very few years the forces of Islam conquered these great civilisations in Syria, Egypt, Persia and Palestine. The third caliph then extended his empire westwards through north Africa, while in the eighth century the Umayyad dynasty of caliphs spread the faith right across into central Asia and western India as well as up into France and Spain. Although Charles Martel drove Islam out of France after the battle of Tours in 732 A.D., the Muslim armies continued to threaten Europe from the east for centuries. The result is that Islam still today reigns supreme in some areas of south-eastern

Europe. Inevitably her military occupation of so many
lands involved also a religious and philosophical encounter
with Zoroastrianism in Persia, Hinduism in India and the
various forms of contemporary Christianity – Nestorian,
Eutychian, Byzantine and Roman.

(b) The Middle Ages

There can be little doubt that the various religions
influenced each other in their developments. Thus Al-
Ghazzali (1059–1111), probably the greatest Muslim
theologian of all time, built his thought on the foundations
of mystic experience and on traditional orthodox Islam. He
also used the Greek philosophy of Aristotle, channelled to
him through Christian Byzantium. He in his turn impressed
Maimonides (1135–1204), the towering figure of Jewish
thought, and also Aquinas (1223–1274) whom Paul Helm,
in the *New International Dictionary of the Christian
Church*, calls "the greatest philosopher and theologian of
the medieval Church". Helm goes on to affirm that "the
influence of Aquinas on Protestantism must not be mini-
mised".

At the time of Aquinas there were also growing contacts
between the two religions through the work of Raymond
Lull (1232–1316). This pioneer Franciscan missionary
among Muslims sensed the need for Christians to develop
an understanding of Islam. He envisaged the establishment
of various monastic and other colleges for the study of the
Arabic language, Muslim art and Islamic theology. He
himself sought to confront the claims of Islam with the
teachings of Christianity.

(c) The crusades

Islam found itself in close contact of a less happy nature
during the first centuries of this millennium through the

crusades. The Christians learned much from their Muslim foes and carried back with them to Europe new knowledge of the sciences, geography and the arts as well as daintier morsels such as sugar, mirrors and cotton. It would seem that Muslims learned little of value from this particular contact with Western Christianity except perhaps a new sense of appreciation for Jews and the Orthodox Christians of Byzantium who suffered equally from the vicious onslaughts of the Christian armies.

Sadly, these first six centuries of close contacts with the outside world gave way to an increasing isolation. Even in the Ottoman Empire the Christians were set apart in self-governing communities and Muslims received little direct influence from them. After some centuries of confident Islamic independence, nineteenth-century colonialism shut the Muslim nations into a ghetto-like sense of inferiority. The frustration of impotent weakness largely cut them off from free intercourse with other religions and philosophies. Of course this is a generalisation. There were exceptional examples of Muslims relating as equals with those of other faiths. But generally speaking, despite the heat of internal revival movements, Islam froze in the refrigerator of isolation.

As we have already observed, Islam today is breaking out of its cocoon. It is having to encounter the realities of life in a world where various philosophies and religions rub shoulders. This is true not only of individual Muslims who travel or who meet foreign visitors to their country, but also of whole societies and nations which face comparison with other systems elsewhere. And the world of mass media ensures that all societies come under international scrutiny.

2 Outside influences
In this chapter I want to look briefly at four outside influences to which Islam is having to react today.

(a)   *Materialism*

Already, after the First World War, the insidious seeds of materialism were eating at the very fabric of Islam. The first outward sign of this was the abolition of the Muslim caliphate in the newly reformed state of Turkey. Legally Turkey became a secular state in which Islam was the normal practice, but civil and legal power moved out from the total control of the religious authorities. At first, secularism was limited to a relatively small number of avantgarde intellectuals, but with the years this small beginning has blossomed into a more widely influential tree. It has not only spread to greater numbers of people in Turkey itself, but also to many other Islamic lands.

Secularism features today not only in the political relationships of state and religious leaders, but also in the sphere of education. Traditional Muslim educational patterns have stressed believing acceptance of God-given theology and ethics, at the expense of a more rational critique which lies at the heart of Western liberal educational forms. This has meant that most Muslims in the past have learned Islamic beliefs by heart without attempting to evaluate them critically. Even in more westernised circles there has still been virtually no criticism of the Quran, although the Shi'ite Indian scholar Sayyid Amir Ali attempted to give a lead in this direction with his highly popular and controversial *Spirit of Islam*. In his book he claims that the Quran was written by Mohammed and not revealed direct from God. It should therefore be read and studied without the traditional interpretations of Muslim religious authorities.

Although such radical views have not yet taken firm root in Islamic circles, the influence of Western critical education is gaining ground insidiously. In their interesting book *Crisis in Muslim Education* Husain and Ashraf grapple with the "conflict between tradition and modernity". They emphasise that Muslim education has achieved "an implicit acceptance" of the fundamental norms of Islamic faith and life. It does not "presume to build up new hypotheses", but rather underlines the preservation of the values of the past. Such "unquestioned acceptance" is today increasingly challenged by Western education. As Husain and Ashraf say,

> The traditional Islamic education system has been superseded by a modern one which has been borrowed from the West. As a result text-books and courses and even methods of teaching are creating doubts in the minds of the students about the fundamental tenets and assumptions of Islam.

Islam today undoubtedly faces a duality in society. On the one side are the old Muslim educational patterns, creating a rigidly traditional faith; on the other are the critical Western forms of education and the more avant-garde modern intelligentsia. Islam cannot remain immune today from the inroads of secular materialism.

Modern entertainments and mass media further erode the values of Islam. Thus in Iran the revivalist Islamic revolution vented its wrath on cinemas with their foreign approaches to sex, women, alcohol and material values. Western television programmes and books contribute to the general onslaught on traditionalism. The revived faith of revealed religion has declared war on all that undermines simple faith in God and his demands.

Western Christianity has faced this tension for a hundred years and has been unable to resolve it altogether successfully. We can only stand by and wonder whether the rather less flexible Islam will prove itself able to reconcile a living faith in God and an acceptance of material advances.

Many Muslims are also wondering whether Islam can

absorb modern technology and commerce without a Western world-view.

The problem is further exacerbated by inherent difficulties in practising the routine life of Muslim prayer and fasting in a non-Muslim society. The Christian knows the difficulty of having a Quiet Time in the rush of modern secular life, but at least the Christian faith has no rigid patterns which ought to be followed. The Muslim is normally expected to pray five times a day unless there are serious and exceptional reasons for not doing so. Likewise the fast month ought to be followed unless it is made impossible by sickness, pregnancy or some such definite hindrance. It becomes exceedingly hard for the ordinary Muslim to stop for prayer in the midst of his daily work in a westernised society. And the diplomat in the United Nations or in an embassy in Paris may not find the fast month easily practicable.

For one reason or another increasing numbers of Muslims yield to the temptations of materialism and secularism. Even in conservative Saudi Arabia visitors may be shocked to see Muslim men flouting the public prayer times, sitting around and gossiping outside while their more devout friends observe the prayer time. The Muslim world may not yet have slipped as far down the secular road as our nominally Christian lands, but the tendency is clear. The threat of irreligious materialism stares Islam in the eyes.

(b)   Marxism

In former years many considered Islam the ideal bulwark against the inroads of Communism. It was thought that Islam's fanatical belief in God could hardly tolerate close association with blatant atheism. History has disproved any such over-simplistic assumptions. Some Communists have managed to explain away the anti-religious stance of Marx,

Engels and Lenin and have affirmed a belief in God. They have maintained that Communist opposition to religion was really only because "the parson has ever gone hand in hand with the landlord" and the Christian Church was always on the side of the "haves" rather than the "have-nots". Hatred of the status quo therefore inevitably meant antipathy towards religion. But, for example, the Indonesian Communist Party in the early 1960s claimed entire agreement with the national constitution's belief in the one God.

For its part Islam has also been able to accommodate itself to the ideals of Communism. The Muslim emphasis on social equality obviously fits a post-colonial situation. Newly independent nations naturally and vehemently dislike imperialism and the class distinctions which so often accompany it. Muslims can therefore easily relate to Marxism. A few years ago this easy relationship between Islam and Marxism seemed to flourish. Egypt and the Arab nations felt a close affinity with the Soviet Union. Russian arms and aid flowed into the area. Still today the former South Yemen, now the People's Democratic Republic of Yemen, manages to combine the two philosophies of Marxism and Islam. Syria and the Palestine Liberation Organisation also maintain a strong Muslim faith together with close political ties with the Soviet Union. These ties have been built on the basis of mutual opposition to Jews and to the State of Israel. But on the other hand there have been difficulties. Egypt moved out of the Communist sphere of influence some years ago, while Sudan and Ethiopia have not been entirely stable in their relationships with the Soviet Union.

There have also been direct confrontations. The ultra-conservative Albania has not hesitated to suppress all religion, including the Muslims. And now we also see Islam and Marxism locked in a bitter struggle in Afghanistan.

Realising the inherent dangers of their position, the Marxist authorities have sought to woo Muslim leaders in Afghanistan, but still the opposing rebels take to themselves the title of "holy warriors". Their name is the present participle of the word for the traditional Muslim concept of holy war, *jihad*. They see themselves as fighting not only for the people of Afghanistan against an invading alien power, but also as the warriors of God against the godless forces of atheism. Other orthodox Muslim groups around the world feel their responsibility to support their brothers in this holy war. It is dangerous to attempt to prophesy the outcome of such bitter battles between Marxism and Islam.

Some onlookers feel that the honeymoon between these two great forces has come to an end. The fundamental disagreement between God-fearing religion and atheism has become plain for all to see. If this proves to be the case, then we may look ahead to increasing antipathy to Marxism in the Muslim world.

Other prophets foresee the *jihad* of Afghanistan spreading to the related Muslim peoples of the Soviet Union. There are approximately fifty million Muslims in the Soviet Union who form about 20 per cent of the total population. They are often of the same tribes as those across the border in Afghanistan. In the early days of the Russian presence in Afghanistan their troops were largely composed of units of Asian Muslim soldiers. After a while these Muslims were withdrawn and replaced by ethnic Russians. We can only conjecture concerning the reasons for this, but all the evidence points to the danger that Muslims could be subverted by their fellow-religionists in rebellion. Muslims may not be too happy to fight against other Muslims, particularly when they are racially related and speak the same language. It has been interesting to note that the Soviet press has begun to complain of interference by the Central Intelligence Agency in stirring up discontent among the Muslims in Soviet Central Asia. We cannot but wonder what the future might hold.

In the past many of the more educated and materialistic students in the cities of Muslim countries were much attracted to Marxist ideology. This was true not only of those students who had been given scholarships to study in Communist countries, but also of those who had imbibed the heady and often Marxist-inspired liberalism of Western education. In the context of anti-Marxist *jihad* in Afghanistan, will such students continue to be attracted to Marxism? If so, will they be increasingly alienated from their more traditionally Muslim societies and even from their political leaders? Will strongly Muslim nations therefore become increasingly unstable politically?

It is clear that Islam today cannot ignore the challenges of Marxism and one of the great open questions for the future must be the relationship between Marxism and Islam.

It should perhaps be noted in this context that both Islam and Marxism have been strongly opposed to the Christian Gospel. While Marxism has often persecuted Christians physically, Islam has usually stifled the Gospel by means of economic and social pressure. As we look back in history, it appears that the Christian faith flourishes better under direct persecution than under the pressures of educational and economic discrimination. Despite fearful problems in such countries as the Soviet Union the Church has maintained a strong witness, but under Islam it has suffered tragic defeats.

(c) Zionism and Israel

Militant opposition to the state of Israel and to the international movement of Zionism has united Muslims all over the world. A common enemy sometimes unites disparate forces more powerfully than theologically more acceptable bases for unity. In our next chapter we shall talk more about the question of Islamic oneness as the people of God, but meanwhile we may note that there is a common mind in vigorous dislike of the State of Israel, although the various Muslim states may disagree on how to combat the enemy.

Opposition to Israel goes hand in hand with support for the Palestinians who in their turn look more widely to the outside world for political help in applying pressure in the United Nations and in economic questions. In this way the Muslim nations find themselves once again in the front line of world politics and thus in close touch with non-Muslim societies.

In many ways Islam and Judaism have much in common. Both stem from the same roots and stress a definite monotheism. In both cases mysticism plays an important part, subject to the overriding emphasis on the revealed word in the Quran and Old Testament Scriptures. These two forms of mysticism differ considerably therefore from some other religions' mystical streams which lack a solid foundation.

Sadly the spiritual and theological affinities between Judaism and Islam cannot result in constructive mutual influence in the political and racial climate of today's world. One suspects, however, that on a personal level there must be some inter-religious friendships in Israel. Hopefully these will bring spiritual impetus, challenge and encouragement across the racial barriers. The enmity between Jew and Muslim ought to compel each to gain some knowledge of the other faith, if only with the aim of opposing and countering it. One can only regret that both Jews and Muslims are often so blinded by prejudice that little real understanding or tolerant appreciation of each other can penetrate.

(d) Mysticism and Eastern religions

A few years ago I was invited to preach at a church in the north of England. Driving through the surrounding housing area towards the church I noted the predominance of shops and cafes with the word "Sufi" in their name – "Sufi cloth shop", "Sufi eating house", etc. When asked about this, the elders of the church denied that there were Sufis in the area and said that their neighbours were Muslims. They evidently did not know anything about the mystical traditions of Islam in the Sufi groups. Actually the earlier waves of Pakistani immigration into Britain often led to the establishment of Sufi groups in homes, because Sufis are less dependent on the leadership of trained mullahs and the building of mosques than are the more traditionally orthodox Muslims. In the early days of Muslim immigration there were no mosques and very few mullahs in Britain.

Who then are the Sufis? Largely ascetics, they concentrate on a life of mystical personal relationship with God. The Sufi watchword is the supposed saying of Mohammed: "Poverty is my pride." Through meditative study of the lives of Mohammed, other prophets and the companions of Mohammed, as well as through their asceticism, the Sufis seek to penetrate beyond the outward attributes of self. They aim for unity with the real inner Self which they equate with the ultimate Absolute. This ultimate reality is sometimes equated with the all-pervading "Light of Mohammed" which Al-Ghazzali called "the Idea of Mohammed". In the Sufi's search for union with the Light of Mohammed he may desire to emulate the *mi'raj*, that visionary experience of Mohammed in which he was transported to the Temple in Jerusalem.

This form of mystical philosophy tends toward a monistic equating of one's self with God himself, which may come very close to the Hindu concept that "all is Brahman". The radical distinction between God and man can be removed, leading to an unchristian understanding of the words "see man and you see God". Some have therefore said of themselves, "I am the *haq*" (ultimate truth or reality). Thus Al-Hallaj, executed in 922 for his ideas concerning man's union with God, said "I am He whom I love, and He whom I love is I". Such beliefs inevitably open the Sufi to influence from other religions, particularly Hinduism.

By the time of Al-Ghazzali the Sufis clashed strongly with more orthodox Sunni Muslims. Not only had Al-Hallaj been executed for his heresy, but also the extreme Malamatiya sect, the so-called "drunken Sufis", scandalised ordinary Muslims by purposely flouting common morals and the laws of Islam to demonstrate their disregard for the opinions of man. Al-Ghazzali acted as a mediator to reconcile the more subjective and spiritual streams of Sufism with the more rigid but orthodox Islamic river. Al-Ghazzali went through a period of deep scepticism and disbelief before "God restored to me these beliefs" through a mystical conversion experience. Shattered by the terrors of the Day of Wrath he fled from all worldly positions and became a wandering Sufi. In his writings he testifies how he gained a new sense of peace through an ascetic and contemplative life in which he abandoned human reason as the basis of faith. Using his ecstatic and experiential knowledge as the foundation, he then built up a fully orthodox Muslim theological structure with the help of Aristotelian Greek dialectic. Particularly through his greatest book *Revival of Religious Sciences* he succeeded in making the Sufi way respectable again in Islam. He brought their insights into mainstream Islam. Through Sufi mysticism it may therefore be possible today for subjective Eastern religious approaches to infiltrate into the very heart of the Muslim world. And it is true that some Muslims today are attracted by the subjective mystical experience of Hindu and Buddhist influences, although they are repelled by the grosser idolatrous forms of those faiths.

Conclusion

Islam has been forced to break out of the isolated shelter of its cocoon. Like a young butterfly it faces the attractions and dangers of the wider world. It confronts secularism, Marxism, Zionism and Eastern mysticism. It also has to relate to its cousin religion, Christianity, with which it has so much in common and yet which it opposes in the struggle for the faith and soul of man.

The very fact that Islam is forced today to interact with the wider world is bound to make some Muslims more open to compare Islam with other faiths and thus consider the claims of Jesus Christ. In our next two chapters therefore we shall look more carefully at Muslim theology, the fortress which the Christian witness has to storm. Only then shall we turn to the problems inherent in the Gospel when preaching to Muslims. This will lead us on to some study of the glories of the Christian Gospel.

2
Islam's Strength

Four hundred million Muslims present the Christian Church with a humbling challenge. With the sole exception of Indonesia, the Muslim communities around the world yield few converts to the messengers of the Christian Gospel. Perhaps because of the daunting nature of the task, relatively few Christian workers are actually engaged in mission work among Muslims. And the casualty rate among such workers is also high. Mission among Muslims demands a high degree of persevering endurance in the midst of indifference, open hostility and usually unyielding resistance to the message of Jesus Christ. In the cheerful exuberance of a Christian fellowship it is easy to sing "all over the world the Spirit is moving"; but in the harsh and rocky reality of a Muslim land the Christian worker can gradually lose any sense of vibrant expectancy. I remember preaching in the open air in a South Thailand village. A large crowd listened intently. Suddenly a man at the back called out "That's right. I believe in that!" My reaction was to assume he was mentally deranged, for Muslims in South Thailand don't come to faith in Christ so easily. I was not expecting people to believe!

After a few years of barren ministry the Christian worker may be tempted away to greener pastures where men and women do turn to Jesus Christ for new life and salvation. Such neglect of the tough task of mission among Muslims may be further supported by modern mission theories which urge Christians to concentrate their energies on "winning the winnable". For one reason or another the fortress of Islam remains intact and stands as a constant indictment of the failure of the Christian Church.

No one can doubt the strength of Islam but the Christian will be aware that our strengths sometimes prove to be the points where we can crack. Thus the superb Christian realities of assurance of salvation and the indwelling presence and power of the Holy Spirit represent enormous strengths in the Christian faith. But sadly it is just in these areas that Christians have not only divided unhappily, but have also gone to extremes which have damaged the life and testimony of the Church. So likewise in Islam the apparent strengths contain within them the seeds of discord and weakness.

In this chapter then we shall look at some of these Muslim strengths which hamper the witness of the Christian, recognising at the same time some of the inherent weaknesses.

1 Islam – the final revelation

"Is your grandfather in hell?" The unbelieving leaders in the city of Mecca trapped the young Mohammed with their trick question. Mohammed knew that his grandfather had died without having accepted him as God's messenger and without having forsaken the old tribal deities with their idolatrous worship. Being as yet inexperienced in the political art of diplomacy, Mohammed gave a direct answer and stated baldly that his grandfather was indeed in hell. The men of Mecca immediately accused him of showing disrespect to his clan background and his forefathers.

When Mohammed first began to receive his revelations in the cave outside Mecca, he thought that he stood in the direct line of succession with Abraham, Moses, David, Jesus and the other prophets. To his distress, however, both the Jews and the Christians rejected him and his revelations. They laughed at the errors they detected in his versions of biblical stories.

Because of these early experiences Mohammed knew the importance of showing that he was not rejecting the traditions of the past or the religious heritage of the Jews and Christians. He did oppose the idolatrous worship of nature spirits and minor deities, but he kept within Islam such old religious forms as the *hajj* or pilgrimage around the great black meteorite stone of the *Ka'ba* in Mecca. He adhered firmly to the Jewish and Christian teaching that revelation comes in written form, that there is personal judgment leading to heaven or hell and that there is one creator God.

So Islam sees itself as the final culmination of all previous revelations from God. Mohammed is called the "seal of the prophets", the last in a long line of God's messengers through the ages. Likewise the Quran is the final revealed book from heaven. Although Islam believes in many earlier revealed books in different languages for different peoples, there now remain only three of those which God caused to descend – the Taurat, Law, through Moses, the Zabur, Psalms, through David and the Injil, Gospel, through Jesus. When a prophet still lives, he has authority as God's messenger and his book must be obeyed by God's people. But when that prophet dies and another messenger of God arrives on the scene, then the authority of the previous prophet and his book is superseded by that of the new revelation. Thus all the contents of the Law, the Psalms and the Gospel are contained in the Quran. Mohammed and the Quran represent God's final revelation, consummating all that was before.

Human nature never likes to descend from the superior to the inferior. We strive constantly for progress. It is therefore hard for a Muslim even to consider the possibility of turning back to a former and inferior religion like Christianity. Just as most Christians do not even think of returning to Judaism, so the Muslim also deems it unthinkable that he might revert to Christianity. As a missionary among Muslims in South Thailand and in Singapore, I have often been told that it is impossible for a Muslim to go back to Christianity. When I have told them that in Indonesia many Muslims become Christians, they have often told me that this cannot be true simply because "Muslims don't become Christians".

Such an assured sense of superiority gives Islam an almost impregnable strength. Today, this assurance is further bolstered by the enormous power and wealth of the Muslim nations. Oil wealth not only affects the realities of politics and economics, but it also undergirds this sense of Islamic confidence. In former years the Western nations enjoyed an apparent economic and cultural superiority which was expressed also in missionary attitudes. Today the boot is on the other foot. Supported by the gushing flow of petro-dollars from the Middle East, Islam can afford to sally forth in mission to the world and can assure its own Muslim populations that Allah really *is* God and that Mohammed is indeed his final and supreme messenger. Christians may feel that a sense of superiority is an unbecoming characteristic, but it does make Islam resistant to the evangelistic onslaughts of the Christian witness.

If however the Muslim meets people of other faiths who are just as good as himself, a flaw might be revealed in his apparent fortress of assurance. Thus the Pakistani immigrant in Britain may be disturbed to find that the Muslim community is reckoned to be socially inferior to others and he may therefore query the validity of his religion. In ghetto-like defensiveness he may be fanatically and rigidly Muslim, but his children may well become open to Christianity and he himself will often have a deep sense of insecurity with regard to his Muslim faith.

2 God is one

When I was doing some study of the Christian doctrine of the Trinity during my theological training, two young Jehovah's Witnesses visited us. In the course of our conversation I challenged them on the inevitable weaknesses which must occur in any faith which lacks a knowledge of God in Trinity. If there is no mediating Son of God, then God must either be stripped of his absolute glory in order to relate to man or he will remain in isolated splendour with such glory that man cannot approach him. And without the Holy Spirit living in the midst of God's people and indwelling the believer, man will be left alone to struggle to follow God and his precepts without the direct aid and presence of God.

Muslims, like the Jehovah's Witnesses, reject the Christian doctrine of the Trinity and affirm the apparently simple doctrine that God is one. Certainly the simplicity of this belief makes it easy to comprehend and is therefore a strength in Islam. As Christians we all know how hard it is to grasp the deep truth of the Trinity – and it is even more difficult to explain it to others. The Muslim has no such problems. He glories in the simplicity of his creed – "There is no god but Allah and Mohammed is the messenger of God."

But in the history of Muslim theology the doctrine of the unity of God has actually presented considerable problems. Theologians have asked whether the attributes of God are eternally one with God. For example, God is merciful. Is mercy therefore an eternal entity? If so, is God unique in his eternal nature? Must the Muslim affirm that through all eternity there has been God and there has also been mercy? Likewise the theologians have recognised the difficulty inherent in the Muslim affirmation that God is all-knowing. How can he be all-knowing if there is nothing to know? If in eternity there has always been something to know, then God is not the only ultimate and eternal being. If however the object of God's knowledge lies within the very being of God, then God is divided within himself. In any case the unique oneness of God must be compromised. With the Christian doctrine of the triune God, no such problems arise: the Father knows and loves the Son; the Son knows and loves the Spirit; the Spirit knows and loves the Father.

In classical Muslim theology the debate concerning the oneness of God has been particularly intense with regard to the Quran. After considerable deliberation, orthodox Islam has accepted the doctrine of the uncreated nature of the Quran. The heavenly prototype, the so-called "Mother of the Book", has existed through all eternity with God. The Quran differs from other created things, for it never was created. The eternal word (an exact replica of the heavenly book) was revealed to man through Mohammed.

The Christian inevitably parallels the Muslim concept of the eternal uncreated word with the Christian doctrine of Jesus Christ, the Word of God who was "in the beginning with God" (John 1:2). Christians have struggled with the relationship between God and the eternal Word of God which became flesh in the person of Jesus Christ. The same basic question faces the Muslim. What is the relationship between God and the uncreated Quran?

The apparently simple doctrine of the unity of God actually presents Islam with serious theological problems. As we shall see later, the lack of a doctrine of the Trinity also makes God distant and unknowable.

3   Islam is one

Oneness, *tauhid*, lies at the very heart of Islamic thought. As God is one, so the people of God are one. Islam strongly emphasises the community of the people of God, the *umma*. At the time of Mohammed the Arabs enjoyed a sense of community and security in their clan structures, but with growing urbanisation society required a new system. Islam provided this by replacing clan solidarity with the religious *umma*. Thus, as Watt has pointed out in his *Mohammed, Prophet and Statesman*, the old caravan-raiding forays by one clan against another were replaced by Muslims warring against infidels.

The deep sense of Muslim unity is strengthened by the knowledge that all one's fellow believers are praying in the same way, at the same time, with the same Arabic prayer formula and all facing towards Mecca. So also at the annual pilgrimage to Mecca all Muslim men from all over the world share the exhilarating experience of processing around the black meteorite stone at the *Ka'ba* together with multitudes of fellow Muslims. All are dressed alike and all share together in the same rituals. Differences of age, colour or education vanish in the visible unity of the people of Islam. Muslim apologists today underline the significance of the fact that Mohammed rode in triumph into Mecca in 629 A.D. together with two black Africans, Bilal and Usama. In so doing he demonstrated the *tauhid*, oneness, of the Islamic *umma*.

By contrast, in the days of Mohammed, the Christian Church was sadly divided. Mohammed must have known of Syriac Christians among his fellow Arabs, Nestorian Persians, Byzantine Orthodox churches, Western European Latin Christians and Egyptian and Ethiopian monophysite Christians who rejected the traditional Christian doctrine that Jesus Christ has two natures in his one person. These various Christian churches rivalled each other with little display of the love of Christ. It is no wonder that the Quran observes that "the sects are divided concerning Jesus" (Sura 19:37).

Still today Muslims accuse Christians of being seriously divided, while they claim that Islam enjoys unity in the *umma*. How important therefore that Christians should display that oneness in love which we preach about in the

Church! In mission among Muslims we cannot afford the luxury of divisive rifts in the Church. The scandal of multitudes of missions along national, denominational or doctrinal lines could be as much a stumbling-block for the Gospel as the message of the cross of Christ.

The community of Islam is not only a religious phenomenon, but also a social entity. To belong to the faith of Islam means that one belongs to a community. The convert from Islam to Christianity needs therefore to join a totally new social grouping. He is likely to be rejected by his family, his friends, his employers and possibly even his government. He will find it hard to gain employment, to find someone to marry or to bury him when he dies. He will therefore have great need of a truly loving and supportive fellowship in the Church of Jesus Christ, which will become his new family. The Kenyan theologian John Mbiti has called the Christian Church "the new tribe"; in Muslim circles we might call it the new *umma*. Unloving empty seats between Christians in church meetings will not help!

Islam is not, however, in any position to throw stones at the Christian Church. Its own greenhouse is no less fragile. Islam too knows the tragedy of divisions. Of recent years the revolution in Iran has alerted the rest of the world to the tensions between the Shi'ites and the orthodox Sunnis. Saudi Arabia and the Gulf States tremble at the threat of the Iranian Shi'ite revolution spilling over into the minority Shi'ite communities in their own lands. Shi'ite Iran has not enjoyed the best of relationships with Sunni Iraq. Likewise in Afghanistan the Shi'ite groups have not found it easy to unite with Sunnis in their joint fight against the Russians. And the Shi'ites are further divided into two main groupings, the so-called "Seveners" and "Twelvers".

Many orthodox Muslims dismiss as non-Islamic the Ahmadiyya Muslims, the followers of the late-nineteenth-century Punjabi Mirza Gulam Ahmad. They have been

outlawed in their native Pakistan as well as in Malaysia and
Singapore. I well remember their mosque in Singapore
being stoned by Sunni Muslims while huge crowds gathered
in a fanatical rally to denounce them as heretics. But their
leader, a fine upstanding man with red beard and flowing
white robes, continued boldly to preach both in Singapore
and in Malaysia. He typifies the missionary zeal of this
movement, which has had considerable success in Britain
and in various other countries. But in 1914 they too split
into two movements.

The unity of the people of Islam is a fine ideal, but it
remains unrealised.

4 Ethics

Islam accuses Christians of allowing moral degeneracy.
They cite debates on homosexuality and the all-pervading
use of alcoholic drink with the consequent spread of drunk-
enness, alcoholism and immorality in society. The Muslims
note the lack of firm and definite moral codes in the
Christian Church. They likewise observe the total absence
of church discipline in many sections of the Christian
Church. In contrast they see man's fundamental need for
specific and definite guidance from God. They therefore
glory in the simple purity of the Muslim *shari'a*, or law.

Some European Christians are prophesying a swing of
the ethical pendulum away from permissive laxity back to
puritanical morality. Others, however, doubt whether
Europeans could ever accept again a rigid moral code
which smacks of legalism. Perhaps both contain an element
of truth, for one cannot generalise for a whole population.
It may well prove true that some people will return to strict
and even legalistic moral systems, while others will continue in reaction against all rigid norms. Certainly today
some sects and branches of the Christian church are rein-
troducing strong authoritarian structures with very definite

rules of discipline, while others still fight all forms of legalism. In such a context could Islam become an acceptable faith because of its strict moral code?

We note again that apparent points of strength contain hidden cracks and flaws. The supposed simplicity of Muslim law and morality stimulates Islamic scholars to profound debate. Four basic schools of law vie for influence in the various Muslim communities. They disagree fundamentally on how to interpret and apply the four *usul*, basic sources of law:

The Quran
The Sunna – words and deeds of Mohammed
The Idjma – the common agreement and traditional practice of the Muslim community
Kiyas – reasonable analogy and comparison with other known laws.

Much debate rages concerning the validity of using *ra'y*, personal judgment, in determining the application of the law. In the Muslim traditions it is said that Mohammed once sent a governor to Yemen and asked him what is the basis for legal judgment. He answered, "The Book of God." Mohammed countered this with the question, "And what if that fails you?" He then replied, "I turn to the judgments of the Prophet." When asked again what he would do if the Prophet's judgments proved inadequate, he affirmed, "I would use my intelligence and not fail."

But debate centres not only on the relationship of revealed law to the use of personal judgment and intelligence, but also to the question of *istihsan* which is the general good of the Muslim community. Thus in an article in *God and Man in Contemporary Islamic Thought* Sheikh Yamani of Saudi Arabia strongly implies that *istihsan* even overrides what may seem to be the word of the Quran or the Sunna. But who judges what is actually for the general good

of the Muslim community? There may be a danger that a
Muslim form of the Leninist "Democratic Centralism" will
give undue power into the hands of a small group of
leaders.

But perhaps the greatest problem in the application of
the Muslim law stems from its relative rigidity. It is not easy
to adapt the law to changing cultural and social environ-
ments. Islamic jurisprudence has however developed certain formulae for maintaining strict loyalty to the traditional authorities while still being able to adapt them to
the world of today. Thus, for example, "patching" allows
the legal expert to extract sections from the various law
schools, put these quotes together and thus form a totally
new law. "Patching" is based on the word of Mohammed
that "the differences of opinion in my people are a mercy
from God."

There remains a distinct contrast between Islam and the
Christian Church. Islam struggles with a relatively rigid
system, finding it difficult to keep it culturally and socially
relevant. Christianity can sometimes lose hold of the solid
rock of an objective ethic because of our understanding
that God's word is always culturally and historically related.

5 Life has no separate compartments

In recent years Christians have been battling against false
dichotomies between the spiritual and the secular. In former times some Christians so emphasised the fact that
Christians should not be "of the world" that they tended to
separate the spiritual life from secular realities. As a result
it became quite normal to be a "Sunday Christian" and still
today some Christians boast that they are not interested in
politics, economics and the affairs of the world. In reaction
against this, many Christians today underline Jesus' words
that his disciples should remain "in the world". As a result

irrelevant spirituality gives way today to the danger of unsanctified relevance.

While it stands clearly in the Bible that the disciples were not taken out of the world and that every area of life comes under the sovereign rule of the creator God, yet God does mark off certain people and things as belonging in a special way to himself – Israel and the Church, the Temple and the Sabbath. The Christian needs to think clearly and biblically on this subject; what is the relationship of the Christian to social and political questions?

Islam allows no radical distinction between the secular and spiritual realms. Mohammed himself became the political ruler of Medina as well as being the great prophet. The title of Watt's book is therefore significant: *Mohammed, Prophet and Statesman*. While it remains true that in the early Muslim States there were commercial and police courts as well as the main religious courts in which the *qadi*, or Judge, administered Islamic law, yet it should be noted that all these courts submitted to Islamic law.

Most cultures outside of Europe and North America believe that life is integrated. Religion cannot be filtered out of the stream of everyday life. The world of the spirit infuses every aspect of life – health and weather, economic, social and political questions, ethical and legal issues. Islam also believes in this cohesive wholeness in life. God rules over all and his laws provide the standards for every question.

At first sight the onlooker may admire such a unity in life. But religious and political leadership do not always go happily hand in hand. Spiritual wisdom does not automatically include political effectiveness. Calvin and Cromwell did not produce political paradises and the Muslim state with Islamic law also seems far removed from the Garden of Eden.

The great Muslim thinker Afghani has said in his *Refu-*

tation of the Materialists that religion is the basis of a nation, its culture and its civilisation. But he also notes that tension inevitably exists between religion on the one hand and science and philosophy on the other. He feels that this tension forms a natural part of human nature in which our spiritual inclinations do not always agree with our intellectual and physical desires. Afghani observes that this tension in man and in society is not only natural, but also creative. He regrets any tendency to break this balance by overplaying the secular and thus becoming so-called progressives, or by retreating into a religious ghetto and becoming traditionalist conservatives. As we observe developments in Iran and other Muslim countries, as well perhaps as the more recent American emphasis on being born again as a desirable precondition for political office, we realise that both Muslims and Christians find it hard to maintain the balance and tension between the secular and the spiritual realms. While Christianity was born in a minority situation and therefore tends to lose its vitality when the Church gains political power, Islam flourishes when it can establish a Muslim state under Islamic law. The Muslim tendency to equate and identify the secular and spiritual realms indistinguishably may prove just as facile and dangerous as the Christian tendency to compartmentalise in a false and exaggerated dichotomy.

Conclusion

Christian witness and mission has hit its head against the strong points in Islam, and has rarely been able to expose the underlying weaknesses. Islam's stark simplicity and assumed superiority have seemed to present the Christian messenger with an unyielding fortress. But the faith of some of the more thinking and educated Muslims has been eroded by wider contacts with Christianity, Western educational systems, materialism and Marxism.

3
Man, Sin and Satan

In all religious discussions there are two fundamental questions: What do you believe about the nature of man? What do you believe about the nature of God? In this chapter we shall look at the Muslim understanding of the nature of man, while in the following chapter we shall see more of Islam's belief about God.

In any discussion on the nature of man we cannot avoid looking at concepts of sin, ethics and the spiritual battle with Satan.

1 Sin

At first sight it would seem that Christian and Muslim teachings converge in that both believe that God created man without sin, but man then fell into sin. But this apparent similarity proves misleading when more closely examined.

Islamic theology has indeed stressed that man was created good, but being made of clay he was by nature weak and fallible. Because of this inherent weakness man succumbed to the temptation of the Devil. Thus weakness and goodness go together in man. The theologian Al-Nazzam taught that faith and unbelief, good and sin are products of the same faculty in man. He therefore denies the Christian idea of man's inner battle between good and evil, for both stem from the same nature and the same free will. As the *Dictionary of Islam* says: "all human actions result from man's free will".

Islam acknowledges the sovereign power of God, but this in no way detracts from the absolute freedom of the human will. The Quran affirms that "God changes not what a people has until they change it for themselves" (13:11). Likewise the freedom of the human will is not denied by any form of the Christian doctrine of original sin. Bevan Jones in his *People of the Mosque* says that "man is by nature weak but not tainted" while in Stanton's *Teaching of the Quran* the author states that man is "created in trouble, being mortal and inconstant when tested with good and evil." The Muslim is deeply aware of his human weakness, but will deny the Christian doctrine of the corrupt nature of man through original sin. Thus in the Islamic conference in Swanwick, England, in 1979, G. Hehmatyar of Afghanistan affirmed in his paper on mission, "No original, inherited sin stands between the individual and his destiny – for *nothing shall be attributed to man but what he himself has striven for*" (his emphasis). Hehmatyar went on to say, "Sin means no more than a lapse from the innate, positive qualities with which God has endowed every human being."

The Muslim will talk more therefore of sins than of sin. The Christian could trim his message to the prevailing winds of Islamic thought. He would then preach a Gospel of God's forgiveness of sins rather than of a regeneration which changes the very heart and nature of man.

It should, however, be noted at this stage that the Sufis, the mystics of Islam, would rather emphasise that it is man as such who is a sinner. Thus Al-Ghazzali himself does not merely talk of man's clay-like frailty. In his essay "That which delivers from error" he states that the human heart has health and soundness together with disease and destruction. Even so, he goes on to say that this disease stems from ignorance of God, disobedience and following selfish desire. He is not claiming sin to be of an inherited nature.

Christian doctrine has always balanced the pessimistic fact of original sin with the positive truth that man is made in the image and likeness of his creator. This image of God has been tragically corrupted by sin, but reformed theology has consistently maintained that some vestiges of that image remain in man. In Islam too man is said to have been made in God's form and thus reflects the very nature of God. Man is endowed with great dignity as God's *khalifah*, or vice-regent, on earth. The Quran even shows angels falling down before man. Islamic theology maintains that being made in God's form we have within us the seven personal qualities of God: life, will, knowledge, power, hearing, seeing and speech.

In sharing the Christian faith with Muslims we shall therefore find clear parallels upon which to build. But it is clear that the Christian message will contradict some aspects of Islam's view of the nature of man.

We shall certainly agree with the positive dignity of man as God's creation and as a reflection of the nature of God. But we shall also want to say that men need the redeeming and regenerating work of Christ. The Christian will feel that Islam's doctrine of man does not sufficiently take into account the reality of a fallen nature and the resultant natural bias towards sin.

The Christian will also want to talk much more about man's innate sin rather than just about weakness and sins. For the Christian, sin causes moral guilt which should lead to fundamental repentance, while the Muslim teaching about frailty and weakness can lead more to an attitude of fatalism.

While we have seen that Islam talks more of sins than of sin, the Quran contains remarkably little definition of sins. It does however have some denunciation of specific sins like pride, ingratitude towards God, coveting or rejection of God. In the Hadith, the Traditions of Islam, Mohammed is supposed to have said that "the greatest sin is to associate another with God", but he then goes on to add other equivalent iniquities such as "to vex your parents, murder, commit suicide, swear or lie."

Although Stanton in *The Teaching of the Quran* claims that "the teaching of the Quran about sin as such is very sparse", the Quran does contain a whole range of words for sin. The most frequently used words (*ithm* and *dhanb*) seem to signify the doing of that which is forbidden rather than anything which is inherently morally wrong. There is however another word (*khati'ah*) which is only used five times in the Quran, but which seems to have the idea of failure to attain God's standards. Its root contains the thought of stumbling or committing error and it is also used of a bowman whose arrow misses the target. But even this word hovers in a cloud of doubt, for Gibb and Kramers in their *Dictionary of Islam* query such root meanings for the word and claim that it merely signifies a sin committed on purpose.

Abu Talib and then Al-Ghazzali were quite definite in cataloguing sins. They divided sins into four basic categories:

Sins of pride
Satanic sins – envy, deceit and other evil attitudes in the
    mind
Animal sins – anger, lust, coveting, etc.
Beasts of prey sins – murder, rape, fighting and other
    acts of violence.

With the Muslim denial of original sin, there arises the problem of when a child's actions can be considered to be sins. In traditional Islam it is normally reckoned that a child does not actually sin until he is twelve years old. After that age he can sin and is therefore also accountable for his actions. On one occasion I asked a Muslim mother of a dozen children whether she found that this Muslim belief fitted her children. She smiled shrewdly and assured me that theology is a man's business!

In our Christian preaching and teaching we shall need a careful definition of what we believe with regard to original sin. Are we just individuals or are we ultimately connected with our forefathers, inheriting much of our nature from them? What then is our connection with Adam and the Fall? We shall also want to discuss why certain actions are considered sinful and that leads us into the whole debate on ethics.

2 Ethics

In the Christian faith, ethics are based absolutely on the character of God himself. The regenerate Christian aims to become increasingly like God. We were created in the image and likeness of God, we are being recreated into that image (Col. 3:10) and we shall finally be perfectly like God. We pattern our lives therefore on his nature. He is love and therefore the Christian takes love as his fundamental calling. In all ethical questions true God-like love is the supreme standard. And love is inseparably paired with holiness, for God is holy. We are called to be holy even as he is holy. Likewise God is good and so we are called to be morally good and upright, trustworthy, truthful and honest. God gives us an example of loving service with unselfish self-sacrifice and so the Christian should model his life on that of the Lord himself. Ethics are grounded therefore not merely on revealed injunctions and prohibitions, but principally on the revealed character and nature of God himself.

There is some slight reference to this approach to ethics

in Islam also, particularly in the concept of mercy. The Quran repeatedly calls Allah "the Merciful" and it could be said that the Muslim likewise is called upon to exercise mercy. Certainly Mohammed himself throughout his prophetic ministry stressed the need to care for the orphan, the widow and the poor. Although the officially prescribed *zakat*, or almsgiving, does not date from the start of his ministry, yet the idea of merciful giving to the needy forms a basic part of his preaching even in the earliest days of his work.

Sadly, however, there appears to be a weakness in the Quranic idea of God's mercy. It states that "the mercy of God is nigh unto those who do well" and that God is "a mercy to believers". Sweetman in his *Islam and Christian Theology* says therefore that mercy is the reward for good deeds because "there is no inward compulsion of grace within the being of God". In the same vein Tritton in his *Muslim Theology* affirms that "there is no graciousness to unbelievers". It may be objected that Tritton overstates his case. The great Muslim commentator Al-Baizawi has said that the word "mercy" "expressed that universal attribute of mercy which the Almighty extends to all mankind, the wicked and the good, believers and unbelievers", yet still the basic Muslim idea of mercy seems to have little relationship to the Christian concept of God's grace. As the *Dictionary of Islam* says, " 'Mercy' is used as of a king exercising the prerogative of mercy but not of a father who suffers with his child and loves him out of his disgrace."

However inadequate the Muslim concept of God's mercy, the fact remains that in this one attribute of God Islamic ethics are based on the nature of God. But in other respects ideas of good and evil stem rather from revealed injunctions and prohibitions. The commands of Allah must be obeyed by men without question. Some critics have likened Muslim ethics to a set of taboos. The key words are *haram*, forbidden, and its opposite, *halal*. The word *haram* also implies that which is separated off from common use (e.g. the derivative *harem*, the area of the house and its inmates which are only for the use of the master of the house and not for common use) and only by implication comes to mean that which is unclean (e.g. pork and other forbidden foods).

Ethics based on commands rather than on the character of God face the constant danger of degenerating into legalism. Muslims, therefore, are particularly prone to this, not only in the realm of morals but also when it comes to religious requirements such as prayer or almsgiving. Prayer easily slips into a mere ritual in obedience to God's commands. It often contains little or no sense of actual communication with God or of giving pleasure to God. The intentions of the heart become secondary to the external movements and words of the established order. This in turn can tend to encourage pride in the human performance rather than loving humility in the presence of a gracious God. In a similar way the established pattern of almsgiving easily gives a sense of self-satisfied pride that one has performed one's duty. It often lacks any real compassion for the poor or love for the Lord. Christians too have not always been immune from this when we have based our codes of behaviour only on the "Do's and Don't's" of Scripture without reference to the nature of God. But the Christian emphasis on the fact that God looks on the heart and not just on our outward actions will be a vital element in our witness with Muslims.

3 Satan

Over the centuries of Christian mission among Muslims, much study has been dedicated to the theology and practice of Islam in order that the Christian witness might understand more adequately how to present his message. But relatively little notice has been taken of what is commonly called "popular Islam". This term describes the common superstitions and religious practices which do not conform with classical Islam. My own experience as a missionary among Muslims follows this same pattern. I went to Asia with no knowledge of even the basics of Islam or of theories of Christian mission in an Islamic context, but had to settle down to read the Quran, study Islam and learn as much as possible from experience. At that stage, however, it never occurred to me to look below the surface at the actual beliefs and fears of the Muslims in that area, although I could not help being aware of the tremendous influence of spirit mediums. I saw the charms round people's necks and the spirit strings round the feet of the children, but was blind to the significance of such occult practices and therefore failed to relate my preaching to the heartfelt needs of the people. As a missionary team we also failed to engage in prayerful spiritual warfare with the spirit powers which ensnared so many of the local population.

An ex-Muslim Egyptian student at All Nations Christian College told me that in her experience every Muslim she knew in Egypt had contact with spirit mediums or other similar occult activities. Recently I revisited South Thailand where I had worked for a few months as a young missionary. In those early days the superb tropical beaches were well populated with children playing by the water's edge and some adults swimming in the beautiful warm water. On this recent visit I found that only the missionaries frequented the seaside. The spirits had informed the people that they were hungry for more drowned souls. People were afraid to go near the water. Likewise the Muslim gardener at the mission headquarters in South Thailand refused to sweep the ground under a palmtree which had been struck by lightning because of the power of the spirits.

I recalled then one evening as a new missionary in the

little town of Sungei Golok on the border with Malaysia. The drums were beating loudly and the music reverberated through the heavy tropical air. We went to investigate. Crowds were gathered in the house nearby where a man lay seriously ill on the floor. The "revolving spirit medium" was in command of proceedings. His unusually long hair hung loosely as he prepared for action to heal the sick man. As the drums beat faster and faster, he began to revolve his head round and round. The tempo increased until his hair spun round at such speed that it was impossible to tell at any moment where it was. It looked to me like a propeller. At the same time his voice boomed out in words of command to the sick man and his family, finally reaching the climax where he summoned the spirits to heal the man. Later that evening when he had returned home I secretly tried to revolve my head at speed to see whether this was possible. I failed dismally!

The missionaries in South Thailand assured me that their main battle was not with Islam but with the spirit world of occult powers.

It would seem that Mohammed did not desire to found a totally new faith, but to purge the already existing religions of Arabia of their bad elements and help people to be sincere and truly God-fearing. Bell, Trimmingham and others have written notable books on the Jewish and Christian backgrounds to Mohammed's life and thought. But much more study needs to be given to the animistic background in Arabia at that time. Clearly Mohammed brought over into his new faith various elements from the old Arab tribal religions. He maintained the practice of the *hajj*, or pilgrimage to Mecca, and the centrality of the black meteorite stone of the *Ka'ba*, which Bell controversially calls an "extraneous chunk of heathenism". At one stage he was even tempted to allow the continued worship of the minor shrine deities who were considered to be the daugh-

ters of Allah. Although he evidently queried the wisdom of
continuing to use the old animistic name "Allah" for God
because of its associations, he did finally take that risk. He
specifically denounced any form of black magic, but never
combated the powerful influence of the *djinn*, spirits, and
other powers.

Still today when Islam converts an animistic tribe, it
begins by allowing many aspects of their old religious life
and practice. Various articles have been written about the
way Islam gradually takes over an African tribe, increasing
the Islamic teaching and content from one generation to
another. Such gradual penetration of a culture certainly
facilitates the spread of Islam, but it also permits the
continuing hold of traditional spirit powers. This is particularly evident in what is sometimes called "shrine Islam" in
Pakistan and elsewhere. Religious practices associated
with the shrines of ancestral heroes and saints give ample
scope for occultism. In Indonesia too, Hinduism and the
ancient Javanese religion are inextricably intertwined with
the faith of Islam.

If the Christian is to be involved in witness among
Muslims he will be wise to pray and think deeply about the
New Testament teaching on the victory of Jesus Christ over
all spirit powers. Sadly this aspect of biblical teaching has
sometimes been neglected in our churches. More recently
its rediscovery has often been linked to religious extrem-
ism. This should not discourage us from a truly biblical
approach to this subject, for without it we shall enter the
battle without adequate spiritual armament. We need wisdom and power in handling men and women whose lives
have been captured by such occult powers.

In Chapter 5 we shall look at certain aspects of the work
of the Holy Spirit; one important endowment of the Spirit is
power. Let us ask the Lord to give us the courage to enter
into the thick of this spiritual battle and not just hover on

the peripheries. We must not sit comfortably in the ivory towers of cerebral theological debate. We need to cry to the Lord for the power of the Spirit through the victorious name of Jesus Christ.

Conclusion
The Muslim and Christian understandings of the nature of man are similar, but differ in vital respects: the concept of original sin is alien to the Muslim, and his response to God is based on obedience to a forbidding rather than a loving authority. The spirit world of occult powers is very much alive within Islam, and needs to be approached with great care.

4
Stumbling-blocks to the Gospel

Islam's resistance to the Gospel of Jesus Christ stems from two sources – the strengths of Islam itself and the real difficulties inherent in presenting to the Muslim the great news of Jesus Christ.

In Chapter 2 we noted some of the strong points of Islam which make it almost impregnable to all attempts at witness. Now we shall look at the other side of the coin. When witness *is* embarked upon, some aspects of the Christian message stick in the Muslim's throat and he finds it hard to allow the Gospel to enter deeply into his mind and heart.

1 The Trinity
I was visiting with a friend an old Sufi leader in his tiny cloth stall in the market. As a mystic of Islam, he longed to share his experience of God with us. This was during a time of political upheaval and revolution. Danger stalked the streets and to be seen associating with Christians or foreigners was almost suicidal. As we had wandered slowly through the old market, other men had greeted us but none wanted to be seen talking with us. But the old Sufi insisted on us sitting with him on his carpet in his stall. He asked me to tell him how I had come to know the living God. His eyes sparkled with joy when he heard that I had experienced the reality of God in my life when I was fifteen years old; he too had turned from a mere book religion to a personal

knowledge of the living God when he was fifteen. He told me how he had been moved through the testimony of his aunt who had become a Sufi.

When I talked of Jesus, he acknowledged the truth that in Jesus we can see God very clearly. Jesus was for him too the way to God.

"You must forgive me," he said. "I cannot invite you to my home to eat and pray together. In normal times I would insist on you coming to my house, for we both love the living God and our hearts are therefore knit together in love. But you will realise that in these days it would be suicide to invite you to my home. Nevertheless we can drink tea together as we sit on the one carpet here. I may be arrested and tortured for this, but I shall probably not be killed."

I was challenged that a Muslim would be willing to pay such a price for fellowship with a Christian believer. How much do I treasure fellowship with my brothers and sisters in Christ?

But could I really enjoy spiritual fellowship with this Muslim? He loved Jesus as prophet. He even followed Jesus as the way to God and the ideal example. But he denied the deity of Jesus as the Son of God and he rejected the atoning death of Christ on the cross. I longed for him to know the fullness of the glory of Jesus Christ and his saving work for us.

This incident made me ask myself a serious question. When did the disciples become Christians? At first when Jesus called them to follow him they seem to have had little understanding of who Jesus really was. They came to love him as a man with all the beauty and perfection of his being, but only gradually did the fuller light dawn on them. Then at Caesarea Philippi Peter voiced their growing understanding, "You are the Christ" (Mark 8:29). In Luke's account Peter calls Jesus "the Christ of God" (Luke 9:20), while according to Matthew Peter's confession was fuller still: "You are the Christ, the Son of the living God" (Matt. 16:16). The common factor in these three accounts is that Peter acknowledges that Jesus is no ordinary man; he is the Christ, Israel's long awaited Messiah. John underlines the gradual process of growing understanding when he records Peter's words "we . . . have come to know that you are the Holy One of God" (John 6:69).

Matthew, Mark and Luke all state that Jesus began to teach his disciples about his coming sufferings and death after the confession of Peter at Caesarea Philippi. In the period of discipleship before Caesarea Philippi the disciples grew towards an understanding of who Jesus was; now they must begin to learn the further truth that Jesus will suffer and die. It seems that this lesson had hardly penetrated their minds when the time came for the crucifixion of Jesus, for they were evidently caught unawares by the tragic circumstances of Good Friday. Likewise the resurrection of Jesus came upon them as a thrilling but unexpected bolt from the blue. One wonders also at what stage they began to expect with faith the coming of the Holy Spirit upon them at Pentecost.

We do not know when the disciples became Christians in the full sense of that word. But we do know that God in his grace led them on gradually from one degree of understanding to another.

Only slowly did the Church grow into an understanding of the fullness of the Christian faith. In the New Testament days the apostles worshipped the one God, the Father, the Son and the Holy Spirit. It took centuries, however, before Christians could formulate any coherent doctrinal statement of their belief in the triune God and in the divine humanity of Jesus.

Because of the Muslim's religious teaching throughout his childhood, the Sufi I have referred to will find it difficult to progress along the same lines as those first disciples of Jesus. Every Muslim knows that Jews and Christians "worship their rabbis and their monks, and the Messiah the son of Mary" (Quran Sura 9:31). They know the words of the Quran that "Never has Allah begotten a son, nor is there any other god beside him" (23:90). Also in the Quran Jesus strongly denies having said: "Take me and my mother for two gods beside Allah" (5:116). The Muslim therefore grows up with these definite ideas about Christians; that we believe in three gods – the Father, the Mother and the Son. He likewise assumes that the Christian concept of Jesus as the Son of God expresses a grossly materialistic idea of God. On meeting with the Christian witness therefore, the Muslim will often attack him on the doctrine of the Trinity and on the divinity of Jesus, the Son of God.

How then can we help the Muslim in this situation?

(a) What does the Muslim believe about Jesus?

We know that the Muslim believes in Jesus as a great prophet. It might therefore be argued that he could easily follow the footsteps of the disciples as they moved from admiration of the human Jesus to a fuller appreciation of the divine nature of Jesus as Messiah. Actually, however, Islam tells us relatively little about the man Jesus. Neither in the Quran nor in the Hadith, the Traditions of Mohammed's words and deeds, does the skeleton of his miracles and his teachings gain the flesh of personal character and reality. In no way can we say then that the Muslim relates personally to the human Jesus.

In the Quran we read of the virgin birth of Jesus, the son of Mary. At his birth he spoke from his cradle and affirmed that "I am the slave of Allah. He has given me the Book and has appointed me a Prophet". (19:30) He proved that he was indeed a prophet of God by fashioning a bird out of clay, breathing upon it and giving it life. In the Hadith various other miracles are mentioned, including the healing of a leper and a man who was born blind. He also "raised the dead by Allah's permission".

Whereas the Quran's picture of Jesus concentrates on him as prophet and not as Son of God, the Hadith adds an ascetic nature to the picture of Jesus. But both agree in denying Jesus' crucifixion, claiming that the Jews "did not slay him, nor crucified him, only a likeness of that was shown to them" (4:155). Most Muslims believe that God caused the Jews to crucify Judas Iscariot, mistakenly supposing that he was Jesus. Jesus was resurrected and "Allah took him up to himself" (4:158). Although J. S. Trimmingham rightly comments that "any idea of Jesus' future coming derives from subsequent interpretation", most Muslims believe that the time will come when Jesus will return to "break crosses, kill swine" and "marry, have children, and remain forty-five years, after which he will die and be buried" (Hadith). In this way Jesus will prepare the way for the final reign of Mohammed himself. As Muhammad 'Ata Ur-Rahim concludes in his final thoughts on the place of Jesus in Islam: "The Way of Jesus, Prophet of Islam, is over. The Way of Mohammed, Prophet of Islam, has begun."

Despite the various traditional beliefs about Jesus, we must conclude therefore that "it is not the case that the Muslim has seen Jesus of Nazareth and has rejected him; he has never seen him, and the veil of misunderstanding and prejudice is still over his face" (Bishop S. Neill, *Christian Faith and Other Faiths*).

(i) Jesus the Son of God   We have noted that the Christian rejects any carnal understanding of Jesus as the Son of God. We do not believe that God literally and physically had a son. Some Christians may even add that the expression "Son of God" is spiritual rather than physical. But what do we mean if we say that Jesus is *spiritually* the Son of God?

Traditional Christian theology has concentrated its attention on proving that the Bible does indeed affirm Jesus to be the Son of God. It then goes on to define the credal statements concerning his divinity and humanity, and how his divinity can be squared with the oneness of the godhead. But relatively little is said about the actual significance of the term "Son of God". It is assumed that this title relates to the divinity of Jesus rather than to his humanity.

In the New Testament, however, it is not easy to know the exact meaning of the title. Clearly it implies authoritative power (e.g. Matt. 4:3,6) and is related also to the Jewish expectation of the coming messianic king (Matt. 16:16; John 1:49), but in Luke's account of Jesus' genealogy Adam is also called the son of God (Luke 3:38). In the Old Testament the people of Israel had been called the sons of the Lord their God (e.g. Deut. 14:1). We are bound therefore to ask whether the title "Son of God" actually refers to Jesus' divine nature or to his perfect humanity. The perfect man Adam, made absolutely in the image and likeness of God, was the son of God. Ideally Israel too was supposed to reflect the glorious perfection and holiness of God in her life and was therefore also called God's child. Jesus "reflects the glory of God and bears the very stamp of his nature" (Heb. 1:3) and is called God's Son. Now all Christians become by faith and new birth the adopted children of God (John 1:12; Gal. 4:5).

The divine nature of our Lord Jesus does not depend on this one title, but is more easily demonstrated biblically by other means – e.g. he takes over the name of Jehovah in the so-called "I am" statements in John's Gospel. The Christian may happily avoid conflict with the Muslim over the hot issue of this title "Son of God". He may readily agree that this expression need not necessarily imply the divinity of Jesus. In this way we may be able to avoid scandalising our Muslim friends before they have seriously

related to the beauty and glory of Jesus. We long for them
to meet with Jesus, see his perfection and realise his saving
power and grace before they have to struggle with the
theological truth of his divine nature.

(ii) Avoid this controversy!   My wife and I faced again and
again questions about Christ's divine sonship in our years of
missionary service among Muslims in South-East Asia.
Heavy and heated theological debate on this topic proved
blatantly fruitless. We longed to avoid such arid arguments,
in which we felt our views were never seriously listened to.
And yet we knew that no Muslim could honestly consider
the Christian faith until his misconceptions were to some
extent cleared away. We seemed to be in a cleft stick.
Either we avoided the issue and left the Muslim convinced
that the Christian faith is grossly carnal and blasphemous,
or we wallowed in the thick mud of fruitless theological
debate.

Happily an alternative way presented itself in the Malay
and Indonesian languages in which we were ministering.
The word for a key was literally "the son of a lock" and
likewise the word for the digit of a finger or toe was literally
"the son of a finger or toe". We used to suggest to our
Muslim friends that we were surprised at such fearfully
gross ideas. Fancy thinking that a lock takes a wife, who
then gives birth to a key! Actually, of course, the term "son
of a lock" graphically describes the intimate connection
between a lock and its key. They may be physically separated with many miles between them, but the one without
the other will still prove deeply frustrating! The term "son
of a lock" merely describes an intimate relationship. So
also the Christian does not believe that God actually took a
wife and she gave birth literally to a son. Jesus is not God's
Son in that sense. But he is intimately related to God.

We realised that this get-out did not in any way adequately describe the relationship of Jesus to God the

Father. But we found it useful to show that the Christian faith is not stupid, blasphemous and unworthy of consideration. If we could stop the Muslim concentrating on theological controversies concerning the Trinity and the divine-human person of Christ, we might open the door for him to progress towards love and faith in Christ like the early disciples had done.

(b) Christianity is credible

So long as the Muslim labours under the misconception that Christian doctrine concerning the Trinity is grossly materialistic and polytheistic, he cannot even begin to appreciate the true claims of the Gospel. Before he can proceed to an understanding of Jesus's nature and ministry, the mists of misunderstanding need to be dispelled.

We can help this process by carefully explaining that we do not believe in three gods. Although the Quran instructs "do not say 'three' . . . Allah is only one God" (4:171), actually the Christian does believe strongly in the unity of God as well as the triune nature of the godhead. We do not believe in what Muhammad 'Ata Ur-Rahim calls "many-god Christianity" (*Jesus, a Prophet of Islam*). Muhammad 'Ata Ur-Rahim typifies many Muslims in assuming that belief in the Trinity contradicts faith in the unity of God. He therefore misuses Athanasius' statement that "there are not three but one God" as proof that the early Christian fathers themselves were not personally convinced of the doctrine of the Trinity.

Just as we shall want to explain the reasonableness of our belief in the Trinity, so also we shall need to help the Muslim to understand that our use of the expression "Son of God" is not grossly materialistic and fleshly. We do not believe that God took to himself a wife and thus had Jesus as his son. Some Muslims accuse Christians of thinking in these very carnal terms.

We cannot expect that the Muslim will easily or quickly appreciate the depths of the Christian doctrine of the Trinity or of the person of Jesus Christ, the Son of God. As with those first disciples of Jesus in the first century, such faith and understanding will normally only come at a later stage in the Muslim's relationship to Jesus Christ. But right at the start of our witness with Muslims we may well find it necesary to show that we are not polytheistic or carnal in our faith, so that the Muslim may feel free to explore Christian truth with an open mind.

(c) Allah's daughters

At the time of Mohammed the various tribes of Arabia shared a faith in a distant creator God called Allah, but much of their day-by-day worship centred on a host of minor deities and nature spirits. These included the daughters of Allah, some of whom were worshipped at shrines in the immediate vicinity of Mecca. Thus Manat, Allah's daughter who was goddess of fate and death, had her shrine between the towns of Mecca and Medina. The worship of Al-Uzza, another of Allah's daughters, found its focus in a shrine between Mecca and At-Taif, the small town with date plantations to which Mohammed first fled when he lost the protection of his clan in Mecca. In At-Taif itself stood the central shrine of the great Allat, about whom there is some controversy as to whether she was the wife or the daughter of Allah.

The idolatrous worship of these minor deities scandalised the sensitive religious mind of Mohammed. He not only objected to the actual idolatry, but was also deeply aware that the worship of Allah's daughters pushed Allah himself into obscurity. He surrendered his life to the noble mission of restoring Allah to his rightful position as the unique God who alone is to be worshipped. No wonder he reacted strongly when he heard that "the Jews say: Ezra is the son of Allah, and the Christians say: the Messiah is the son of Allah" (Quran Sura 9:30). With his background experience of Arab worship in which Allah was so sadly obscured through the cult of his daughters, Mohammed assumed that a Trinitarian religion would likewise diminish God. No wonder he attacks those "who say: Allah is the third of three" (5:73). It seems clear that Mohammed had little idea what true Christians actually believe concerning the Trinity. The vast majority of Muslims today are no better informed than was their Prophet. In the first stages of Christian witness to a Muslim we need to make it clear that our faith is in no way related to the grossly carnal views which rightly angered Mohammed. Our beliefs also strongly oppose all idolatry and any religious form which pushes God himself into the background.

2 Corrupted Scriptures

It would seem that Mohammed originally thought of himself as being in full agreement with the Jews and Christians in their God-centred faith. In practice however it soon became apparent that neither he himself nor his message was going to be accepted by either Jew or Christians. Mohammed therefore changed the direction of prayer from Jerusalem to Mecca, the Saturday day of rest to the Friday day of prayer and the Jewish *shofar* or ram's horn to the call to prayer by means of the human voice. This symbolised the clear break between the new faith of Islam and the former religions of Judaism and Christianity.

But the relationship between the new religion and its predecessors remained ambivalent. On the one hand we have observed definite opposition with strong rejection of Jewish and Christian beliefs. On the other hand Muslims respect Jews and Christians as "people of the Book" who do not follow the idolatrous practices of other religions. I learned this from personal experience when I was a missionary in South Thailand. One day a leading Muslim came to the house where I was staying and began a speech of deep respect for me as a "man of the Book". After several minutes of flowery speech he solemnly unwrapped the immaculate white silk cloth from around his Quran. He then proffered the Quran to me with the words: "As a sign of my respect for you as a man of the Book, I offer you my Quran. You may kiss my Quran."

On the other hand Islam denounces Jews and Christians because "they perverted the words from their places and forgot a portion of what they were reminded of" (5:13). We stand accused of corrupting God's word. What is the basis for this accusation?

(a) Muslim views of revelation

Until we have some knowledge of Muslim beliefs concerning revelation we cannot really understand the basis of their criticisms of Christianity. When we have examined Muslim attitudes to the Scriptures, then we can see why they accuse us of having tampered with or lost the original revelations from God. This is of course of fundamental importance, for the Christian bases his knowledge of Christ and therefore of the Father on the Bible as the Word of God. If our Bible is rejected as a merely human corruption of the true Word from God, then the clarion call of Christ becomes a shaky whisper.

In his *The Word in the Experience of Revelation in the Quran and the Hindu Scriptures* A. Crollius examines the various words used in the Quran to describe how God reveals his word to men. He shows how these words describe speaking and hearing rather than writing. God's word is written in Arabic in heaven, but it is only spoken and heard on earth. The Quran only talks of men writing in the context of forging false revelations (e.g. 52:41; 68:47). Nevertheless, later developments of Muslim theology have come to accept that God's revelation must not only be written in heaven, but then also put into writing here on earth.

From the earliest times, however, Muslims have been agreed that the Quran was initially written by God in heaven and was then revealed through the archangel Gabriel to Mohammed. Therefore the Quran affirms that "a scripture has come from God" (2:89) and that God has "sent down to you the scripture with the truth" (5:48). God's revelation is also said to be God speaking "from behind a veil", which the great Muslim commentator Baizawi says "is an indication of the letting through of a vision, not of its being withheld".

So Islam believes in a revelation which is already written on a "heavenly prototype". The Quran is a perfect replica of that eternal word in heaven.

Islam uses two distinct words to describe the process of revelation. *Wahy* signifies what we have just described, namely a revelation from God through the archangel to a prophet who then passes on the word to his people without any interference. *Ilham* on the other hand describes a revelation without angelic mediation and with direct human involvement in the shaping of the word. *Wahy* is totally perfect, for it is free from any human error; *ilham* however is partly shaped by men and therefore must be to some degree imperfect. The Quran was revealed in absolute perfection, while the Hadith Traditions come through men and may contain some error.

We notice the significance for the Muslim that Mohammed was said to be illiterate. If he could not read or write, he could not have played any formative role in shaping the revelations which God caused to descend through him. Historians may query whether Mohammed was in fact illiterate, but Muslims will continue to stress this as truth because of its importance for the Islamic doctrine of revelation.

(b)   Christianity and revelation

We realise from the above that the Christian view of
revelation differs markedly from that of Islam. We do not
believe that the Bible was written on a tablet in heaven and
then revealed to man verbatim in the exact heavenly form.
The Christian is therefore not specially concerned with the
actual writing and the shape of the letters, for we are
interested more in the *message* of God's word. The Muslim
maintains that a translation of the Quran into some non-
Arabic language no longer qualifies as the Quran, for it is
no longer a replica of the heavenly word. The Christian on
the other hand will happily use translations of the Bible,
although he realises that he may need to check in the
original language to assure himself that the translation
gives the true meaning.

The Christian faces real problems with these two words
wahy and *ilham*. Neither fits the Christian doctrine of
revelation. In Malaysia and Indonesia Bible translators
disagreed over which word to use for "reveal" in the Bible.
One translation used *wahy* while the other preferred *ilham*.
Both need considerable teaching if they are to be rightly
understood from a Christian point of view. The Bible is
revealed through men who play a vital role in forming the
contents of the books they write. The personality and
background of the writer deeply affects the contents of the
message. Thus it would have been impossible for Moses to
have been the author of Luke's Gospel or for Paul to have
written the prophecy of Amos. Each writer stamps his own
character on the book he writes. And yet we still claim that
what they write is God's word to man and thus shares the
same divine-human nature of Jesus, the living Word of
God.

Christian revelation is not *wahy*, for its writers are not
mere channels who have no influence on the form of
what they write. Likewise the Bible cannot be called *ilham*,

for it is the Word of God and is therefore utterly to be trusted.

(c) Where is the Gospel?

We have seen that the Muslim believes in the Injil, or Gospel, as one of the books which were written in heaven and then revealed through God's prophets. God caused the Gospel to descend through the prophet Jesus.

But when the Muslim begins to read the New Testament he finds the first four books are descriptions of the Gospel written by Matthew, Mark, Luke and John. He then asks where the actual Gospel is. He does not want Matthew's version of the Gospel; he wants the actual Gospel which was in heaven with God and was then revealed through Jesus. The Muslim is looking for God's message through Jesus, not a man's account of Jesus himself. No wonder he accuses the Christians of having lost the original Gospel.

This accusation is further confirmed when he reads in the margin of the Bible that there are alternative readings of certain verses. Different old manuscripts allow various possible versions. But the Muslim view of revelation makes him look for the actual words which God revealed. The Christian is unable to produce what the Muslim demands. So the Muslim cannot understand how the New Testament could be a form of revelation. Contradictions between the Quran and the New Testament further push him towards the conclusion that Christians have corrupted their Scriptures.

We noted earlier the problem that with a Muslim our Christian witness comes up against complex theological questions with regard to the Trinity and the person of Jesus. We realised that such deep issues should not be debated before the enquirer has been attracted to Jesus himself. Now likewise we see that the Muslim enquirer needs careful explanations of the Christian doctrine of revelation before he may be open to allow the Bible to speak to him. It is not easy to face theological teachings which differ radically from those with which one has grown up. Once again we face a real hurdle which can stand between the Muslim and faith in Christ.

As so often in Christian mission we are confronted by the apparently insuperable nature of the task. We grasp like drowning men at every straw of an answer. Yes, it is true that Luke's Gospel has close parallels with Muslim teaching about Jesus and the Muslim may therefore like to read it. Yes, the Bible is the Word of God and does have an unparalleled power to attract men despite their prejudices. But ultimately we have to confess that "apart from me you can do nothing" (John 15:5) and then pillow our despondent heads on the equally sure truth that all things are possible to him who believes. Faith can move mountains.

Despite the undoubted difficulty surrounding our belief in the Bible as God's revealed Word, the history of Christian mission among Muslims shines with glorious examples of men who have read the Bible and been marvellously attracted to Jesus. In Singapore and Malaysia we distributed many portions of Scripture which just contained one miraculous healing story from the life of Jesus. Again and again people were impressed by the very caring attitude of love which the Lord showed when he healed someone. Admiration for Jesus is a good beginning on the road to saving faith.

(d) Jesus, the Word
In the Quran Jesus is called the Word of God. It is true that a similar title is also given to Moses and others. The Arabic *kalimat*, word, denotes a word of authority which sends a messenger from God to men. This word prods man to respond in faith or in rejection and thus leads naturally to

the climax of judgment. In some ways it might be claimed that all Muslim prophets could be called God's Word, but the Quran gives this title in a special way to Jesus.

Many Christian witnesses among Muslims rightly use John's Gospel with its reference to Jesus as the Word of God. The prologue to John's Gospel is indeed very apt with reference to Jesus in the context of Islam. Over the centuries Muslim theologians have debated fiercely about the Quran. Is the Quran eternally with God in heaven? Yes! Is the Quran therefore uncreated in its perfection? The orthodox Muslim answer to that question is also "Yes". The Quran was eternally with God even before the creation of the world. The Quran always was, it was never created. The Christian quotes John's Gospel in order to demonstrate the same truths with regard to Jesus. He always was and He is the eternal Word who was with God before all time.

We may be tempted to think that the Christian-Muslim parallels lie between Jesus and Mohammed, and between the Bible and the Quran. However obvious those parallels may appear, the truth remains that we should actually compare Jesus to the Quran. In Islam the will of God is revealed in the Quran, while in Jesus Christ we have the revelation of God himself.

3 They don't think!

In the past some Europeans have talked of "Mohammedanism", but we need to be aware that Muslims themselves strongly reject this name. They insist that they are not just following Mohammed, for he is not the centre of their faith. He merely acted as God's messenger to call his people to submit to God himself. From the very outset of his ministry Mohammed felt himself to be God's instrument in bringing his people to follow the ways of God.

The first two revelations which he received are recorded

in Suras 96 and 74. In Sura 96 God instructed Mohammed to "recite". The word used has the same root as "Quran" and was used also for the reciting of the Bible readings in the Syriac Christian churches of that time. It therefore implies that the revelations received by Mohammed contain within them the same undoubted authority as the Bible. In Sura 74 Mohammed is commanded to "rise and warn". His message allows no debate. It challenges to decision. Disobedience will result in judgment. God warns his people through Mohammed to submit to the ways of God or pay the penalty.

So it is that the heart of Islam is submission to Allah and his commands. This is demonstrated also in the ritual prayers in which the climax is the act of prostration before God: we have all seen pictures of long rows of Muslim men kneeling before God with their foreheads touching the ground. Gratitude, love, worship – these are the attitudes which mould the character of the true Christian's relationship with the God of grace, love and holiness. As we shall see more fully later, the God of Islam does not relate intimately with his people. Their relationship with him is characterised rather by submission to his power and authority.

In the Bible God calls appealingly to his people: "Come now, let us reason together" (Isa. 1:18). Jehovah does not demand instantaneous obedience and submission without the possibility of reasonable consideration of God's demands. So Job uses the same word as Isaiah in wanting to "reason with" God (Job 23:7). In the midst of his traumatic troubles Job longs to find the Lord and lay his case and his complaints before God. He expects God not only to hear what Job says to him, but also to answer and speak to Job (23:2–7). In the New Testament also the Christian will experience that good, acceptable and perfect will of God when his mind is renewed (Rom: 12:2). The God of the

Bible expects his followers to use their minds. We are to love and serve the Lord with a worship which is intelligible and reasonable (Rom. 12:1).

This biblical emphasis on the use of reason stands in sharp contrast to the Islamic underlining of submissive obedience. We may illustrate this by contrasting the naming of the animals of the earth in Muslim and in biblical tradition. In the Bible God commands Adam to give a name to each type of animal as they parade before him. In Islam it is God himself who gives them their names, while man is merely taught the names which God has commanded. God trusted Adam to use his intelligence and initiative. It is true that Adam's mind at that time had not yet been corrupted by sin, but still today the Christian has the responsibility to use his redeemed powers of reasoning in his love, worship and service of God.

In Islam the unquestioned authority of God is transmitted down into a society based on submission. Whereas the Christian expects to apply his critical faculties to his reading of the Bible, the Muslim will be encouraged to learn the Quran and obey God's word without question. Still today, despite the growing influence of rationalistic humanism and modern education, the Quran has not been subjected to anything like the critical examination which has assailed the Bible. Generally speaking it remains true even today that it does not occur to the Muslim to apply rational criticism to the Quran.

But actually much of the day-to-day Muslim faith depends rather on the traditional teachings of Islam than on the Quran itself. In this Islam is far from unique. Judaism too exalts the Bible in theory, but actually study is centred on the Talmud and rabbinic traditions. And the Christian Church also faces the same danger of saying that our supreme authority is the Bible whereas in practice we often uplift the sanctity of our particular traditions.

And so it is in Islam. The traditions of Islam give the essential teaching even on the five "pillars of Islam" – the Muslim creed, the five daily times of prayer, the compulsory *zakat*, almsgiving, the fast month and the pilgrimage to Mecca. In theory these traditions of Mohammed's words and deeds do not contain the same authority as the Quran itself, but actually their authority is in practice unquestioned. Likewise the Muslim will submit without question to the authority of the traditional schools of Muslim law.

In a strange way too this authority filters down to the leaders of each Muslim community. Their word carries enormous weight as the very representatives of God in upholding the truths of Islam. It is hard to say exactly which leaders hold sway, for Islam is not a hierarchical religion. We cannot really say that the State authorities have the right to determine what is right or wrong. Likewise the religious authorities in the mosque or in the Islamic law schools are not hierarchically above their fellow Muslims. And yet authority is vested in these men and together they wield unquestionable power.

As was sometimes true in Western countries a century or so ago, so in Islam parents retain controlling power over their children even when the children are mature adults. Thus a friend of mine told me recently how she had asked a Muslim fellow student about her Islamic faith. Her friend confessed that she actually knew almost nothing about Islam, but she was a strong Muslim because her parents desired this.

Despite this strong emphasis on unquestioning submission to the authority of God and Islam, yet there is also another traditional stress on the rational use of the intellect. From early on in the history of the development of Islam, some leading Muslims were attracted to Greek philosophy and its use of logic in rational argument. Al-Ghazzali himself was deeply influenced by Aristotle's use of logical debate in his discussions on truth. Tragically this stream of influence in Islam has often been allowed to dry up, allowing the more arid sands of traditional authority to take over.

The very words "Muslim" and "Islam" indicate the predominance of the concepts of authority and submission. Both stem from the Arabic root *aslama* which means to submit. "Islam" is the infinitive of this root, while "Muslim" is the present participle and thus indicates the one who submits.

If Christian witness is to make any impression, it depends on the possibility of rational discussion. The Muslim who submits uncritically to the authority of Islam will not even consider the claims of the Christian faith. We have already noted some of the grave misunderstandings which the Muslim may entertain concerning the Christian faith. Unless therefore the Muslim is willing to give serious attention to the Bible and approach the message of Christ with something of an open mind, he is very unlikely indeed to be converted. The patterns of authority in Islam bind him to such submission to the Islamic faith that he cannot really delve into the mysteries of Christ – and so Jesus Christ remains a mystery to him.

In the more rationalistic and open environment of the West many young immigrant Muslims become dissatisfied with traditional demands for unthinking submission. The Christian emphasis on the use of the informed mind can then prove very attractive. The Christian God trusts us to think!

4 Death to apostates!
Tertullian said: "the blood of the martyrs is the seed of the Church" – but it has not proved true in mission among the Muslims. The threat of martyrdom has strangled the Church.

In the second century the Church in North Africa suffered very considerable persecution and martyrs freely gave their lives for the sake of the Gospel. The great North African theologian Tertullian may well have been influenced by these martyrs in his own conversion to Christ. Certainly he wrote a work called *To the Martyrs* in which he seeks to encourage those who suffer for the Lord in prison. Likewise his *Flight in Persecution* discouraged any unspiritual avoidance of martyrdom.

In Tertullian's own day the Church in North Africa was both large and strong. In the history of the Christian Church it has frequently proved true that persecution of strong churches has led eventually to the purifying of the Church and thus finally to the growth of the Christian community. In such contexts Tertullian's word is true. The spilt blood of martyrs may well prove to be the seed of the Church. But history through the ages has also shown that the persecution of weak or very small groups of Christians has often erased all Christian presence in the area. North Africa itself is a case in point. During the centuries of Muslim rule there have arisen occasional small Christian groups and some individual Muslims have been converted, but again and again the converts have disappeared or have been killed. The blood of the martyrs has not been the seed of the Church. The Church has gone out of existence and Christian witness has had to begin again from scratch.

The law of Islam decrees death to apostates. In some areas today (e.g. Europe and parts of Indonesia) this law has grown slack and it sometimes even proves possible for converts from Islam to remain within their families and communities. A British Pakistani friend of mine was not only able to keep her family ties, but her parents even asked her to help them celebrate Christmas in a British and Christian way. They were living in England and so felt this to be a good and right thing to do.

But in more strongly Islamic lands it can prove suicidal to leave Islam and be converted to the Christian faith. I have written elsewhere of three Muslim girls in Malaysia who were poisoned to death by their mother because they showed interest in Christianity. A Muslim police sergeant in Singapore also knew the danger of murder if he became an open Christian. When I urged him to become a Christian, he asked me poignantly: "Martin, do you want me to be killed?"

Both in Malaysia and in Singapore the Malay race remains solidly Muslim. Chinese and Indian churches abound, but they are culturally alien to the Malays. How can we form significant Christian groups and churches for the Malays when young converts are killed? And because of the danger of death other converts flee the country or find refuge in living anonymously in Chinese or Indian areas. This problem applies equally to such countries as Pakistan and the Sudan, where the relatively large Christian churches belong to different communities from their Muslim neighbours. In the Sudan the Christian Church represents the African-stock peoples of the south, while the racially distinct northerners follow the faith of Islam. In Pakistan the Church uses language and vocabulary carried over from Hindu backgrounds. The Muslim feels alienated by such language and differs from his Christian compatriots both culturally and socially. In a later chapter we shall look more closely at some of the implications of this for the formation of a Christian Church in which the Muslim convert can feel at home.

The Christian Gospel will only penetrate Muslim communities when there are living Christian churches which can have a culturally relevant witness to Muslims. Some of the churches of Indonesia offer us an example of this. An Indonesian may feel as much at home in the Christian Church as he does in Islam, for both are fully indigenous and belong to the land and culture of Indonesia. The Muslim convert can therefore fit easily into a new Christian community and find companionship, identity and support. This is unfortunately not often reflected in the ancient churches of Egypt and Lebanon, which have generally grown culturally apart from the Muslim population. But at least those ancient churches do offer Christian communities into which the Muslim convert can go for shelter and support. In the solidly Muslim nations of the Arabian peninsula and some North African countries there may be no churches at all to receive the Muslim who desires to accept Jesus as Lord and Saviour. And if the occasional convert is speedily martyred, no such community of Christians can develop.

5　Is Christianity Western?

What other stumbling-blocks prevent men from accepting salvation through Jesus Christ? Paul is anxious lest our determination to be free from the trammels of legalistic taboos may so offend people that they will not turn to Christ (Rom. 14:13; 1 Cor. 8:9). And it remains true today that some Christians refuse to limit their freedom for the sake of their Muslim neighbour. They insist on exercising their right to eat pork and drink alcoholic drinks. This adds unnecessarily to the unavoidable stumbling-blocks to the Gospel. As Paul and Peter observe, the very person of Jesus Christ may prove objectionable to some and therefore be a stumbling-block (Rom. 9:32; 1 Pet. 2:8), and the message of Christ crucified may scandalise the Gentiles and block the Jews from faith (1 Cor. 1:23). And how true it is for Muslims, as we have noted, that the Gospel of the Cross seems offensive and blasphemous.

But sadly the Muslim may actually find these relatively minor stumbling-blocks in comparison with the scandal of a Gospel which appears to be a Western import, an imperialistic imposition. This is of course true not only for Muslims, but also for many other people in the lands of Asia and Africa. For some Muslim immigrants in Europe the association of the Gospel with Western culture may prove disastrous, while others will be drawn toward Christ for this very reason. Some European Muslims fear the loss of their national and cultural identity. They will resist the Christian faith and cling firmly to Islam. Others want to become fully British and escape the narrow confines of their ethnic community.

Dressed in Western cultural forms and philosophically foreign theological systems, the Christian faith is tainted with the brush of colonial imperialism. Christian missionaries need to be humbly sensitive as they strive to avoid anything which smacks of Western domination. We long that men and women of all races should have no unnecessary hurdles to surmount in their quest for life and salvation in Jesus Christ. The one and only stumbling-block should be Christ and his death on the cross.

It is tragic that Muslims still often associate the Christian faith with Western society. They observe the apparent breakdown of European cultures and the blatant toleration of sin and immorality. These social evils are associated in their minds with Christianity; that is how Christians behave. They demonstrate little comprehension of the distinction between true Christians and those who may be called "nominal Christians". Neither do they understand that the lands of western Europe are in no sense Christian nations, for neither our governments nor the majority of our populations attempt to submit to Jesus Christ as their Lord and guide. Because Islam brings religion and politics into one indivisible unity, Muslims assume that the same must be true also of Christians. They therefore judge Christ by the national life of European and North American countries.

Historically the link between the Christian faith and Western nations showed itself specially in the crusades. Although Christians may have forgotten the crusades in the mists of long past history, Muslims and Jews cannot so easily allow those tragic episodes to slip into oblivion. The warriors of the Cross raped Jewish girls in such large numbers that Jewish law had to be changed. No longer is one reckoned to be a Jew if the father is Jewish, but today one's race is officially determined according to one's mother. In this way the Jewish community gave relief to the girls who suffered at the hands of the crusaders. And Muslims too fought for their lives against the vicious onslaughts of these same crusaders in a whole series of bloody campaigns.

It should perhaps be pointed out in this context that Christians today are singularly unwise if they use terms such as "crusade" or "crusaders" in areas where they may encounter Muslims or Jews. I was shocked recently to receive a letter from a missionary in a largely Muslim country. The missionary signed his letter: "Yours crusading for Christ among Muslims . . ."

Islam appeals to Africans and Asians as an ally against the domination of Christian Europe. For a Muslim to become a Christian therefore may imply that he is ranging himself alongside the forces of discredited imperialism. National pride will militate against such a possibility.

The Christian witness faces not only the stumbling-block of the person of Christ and his cross, but also must surmount the hurdle of the Gospel being associated with Western Europe.

Conclusion

Islam stands strongly against the Christian Gospel and seems impregnably resistant to all attempts at Christian witness. We have noted the apparent strengths within Islam itself and now also some problems in Christianity which may prevent Muslims considering the claims of Jesus Christ. Some readers may be feeling that the task of mission among Muslims is hopeless, but in the coming chapter we shall see that the Christian has indeed very much to offer to his Muslim friend. And then in the following chapter we shall examine different approaches by which, with the power of the Holy Spirit, we may introduce Christ to the world of Islam.

5
What Has Christianity to Offer?

In this chapter we shall look at a few great truths which turn the Gospel from merely another religion into genuine good news which must be shared. I sometimes wish that we could ditch the jargon word "Gospel" and only use the native English equivalent, for then we might be more forcefully reminded that God has given us a message for the world which is truly "good news".

If we believe that the person and work of Jesus Christ is indeed glorious good news, then in love we cannot keep the message to ourselves. If we truly love our neighbour, we shall want to share that most precious possession with him. And when we see the tragic miseries and disorders of people and societies without the love of Christ, surely we must long to be able to introduce them to the Saviour who can bring new life and new hope both to the individual and also to whole societies.

Biblically, too, the God who created all people and all things desires to be in practice the acknowledged Lord of all. His kingdom does rule over all, but sadly his rightful rule is usurped by Satan, the "prince of this world". Men fail to recognise the authority and rule of God. Only by faith in Jesus Christ and through new birth can men see the kingdom of God (John 3:3) and thus rejoice in the Lord's sovereign rule. The God of creation longs for all men of all races and religious backgrounds to acknowledge his rightful rule and receive all his gracious gifts of life and salvation. The good news of Jesus Christ needs to be preached to all men everywhere, including those within the community of Islam. Even when the way proves rugged, our responsibility lies in a persevering witness which does not turn back in faithless frustration.

1   A Gospel rooted in history

Ever since C. H. Dodd published his influential examination of the apostles' evangelistic messages in the Book of Acts, it has been customary in one way or another to look for a synthesis of the contents of the apostles' sermons in order to determine the core points of the Gospel. But on reading the Book of Acts, we observe that the contents of the messages vary slightly according to the context in which they were preached. Biblical truth is never unrelated to the needs and situations of those who hear God's word.

To gentile audiences the apostolic word includes the foundational fact of the "living God who made the heaven and the earth and the sea and all that is in them" (Acts 14:15), "the God who made the world and everything in it" (Acts 17:24). From this fact of creation Paul deduces that men of all nations should worship the one God and not bow down to mere created objects or idols.

But in preaching to the Jews the apostles did not need to reinforce their already firm belief in the one creator God. The Jews knew that Jehovah was the unique God who had made the world and all that is in it. Likewise in preaching today to Muslims we can follow the apostolic pattern of omitting this great truth, for Muslims too have no doubt in their minds that God is one and that he is the great creator of all.

In their messages to Jewish audiences the apostles strongly emphasised the historical person of Jesus and the undoubted facts of his death and resurrection. The claims of the Christian faith do not depend on some debatable revelation from heaven, but are firmly rooted in the sure facts of history. The Christian message not only comes through a historical messenger, but the actual historical facts of the incarnation, death and resurrection of Jesus Christ form the very heart of the message. Faith in the revealed word from God can therefore be supported and undergirded by the demonstrable events of history. The writers of the four Gospels and the Book of Acts strongly emphasise this historical nature of their message by such expressions as "in the days of Herod, king of Judea, there was . . ." (Luke 1:5) and "this was the first enrolment, when Quirinius was governor of Syria" (Luke 2:2). The genealogies of Jesus in Matthew 1:1–17 and Luke 3:23–38 further underline this.

When I was working as a missionary among Muslims in South Thailand I learned in a new way the significance of these genealogies. On one occasion I gave a copy of the New Testament to a Muslim religious leader. Some time later I revisited him in order to see how he was getting on with it. When I asked him how he was enjoying the New Testament, he replied, "This book has the ring of truth about it." I agreed! When asked further why he thought the New Testament seemed true, he commented that the genealogies showed without question that the contents of the book contain historical truth. He felt therefore that he could trust this book. At that stage he had not read enough to know what the New Testament actually does teach. He had not yet realised that its contents might contradict the faith of Islam, but at least I knew that he would now approach the Word of God with a willing openness.

As we continue in this chapter we shall look at various elements in the glorious Gospel contained in the pages of the Bible, but at this stage we should note that the apostles' evangelistic sermons in the Book of Acts concentrate on the person of Jesus Christ and on his work on the cross and in the resurrection. The Muslim will not often be converted through anything except the attractive perfection and love of the person of Jesus Christ. In our witness with Muslims we must talk much of Jesus, resisting all pressures to engage in mere theological debate.

(a) The person of Christ

True doctrine, sound apologetics, relevant applications, ethical and social implications of the Gospel, the vital nature of prayer or the authority and reliability of Scripture – all these form vital parts of our message, as do many other aspects of Christian truth, but we must not allow any of them to outshine the Lord himself. It is Jesus himself who attracts. He alone saves, redeems and gives new life. In him alone are to be found all the glories of the Christian life and faith. He alone will satisfy the heartaches of mankind and in our evangelism we shall find that only he can attract men like a magnet with the sheer beauty of his person and utter holiness of his nature. His steadfast and deep love can draw men to himself and thus through him to the Father. And his love can change the very depths of our personalities. No wonder that the climax of the apostles' message was "this Jesus" (Acts 2:36), "the Righteous One" (Acts 7:52).

(b) The cross

The Christian Church has developed the cross as the symbol of the Christian faith. The very use of the English words "crux" and "crucial" reveal the significance of the cross for us as Christians. Jesus himself looked forward to his death as the great purpose for which he had come into the world. Jesus came "to give his life as a ransom for many" (Mark 10:45). From the day of his baptism throughout the whole of his earthly ministry his eyes were set on the goal of the cross. Nothing could prevent him from setting his face to go up to Jerusalem to be betrayed and crucified for the salvation of his people.

In John's Gospel Jesus uses the enigmatic expression "my hour" to signify that his death on the cross represented for him the great climax of his life and ministry. In talking of his impending death he exclaims "the hour has come for the Son of man to be glorified" (John 12:23), for he knows that on the cross he will achieve his ultimate victory over sin, death and Satan. In the victory of the cross he parallels the grain of wheat which through death does not remain alone, but "bears much fruit" (John 12:24).

The cross may prove to be a grave stumbling-block to Muslims at first, but they will only be attracted to Jesus when they grasp the glorious significance of the cross which buys for us all the gift of eternal life, an open door to a new relationship with God and all the outworkings of redemption.

(c)   The resurrection

In his preaching to the gentile audience at Athens Paul evidently so stressed the resurrection of Jesus that people thought he was bringing to them two new divinities, "Jesus" and "Resurrection". The resurrection was so central in Paul's thought that he could say to the Corinthians that "if Christ has not been raised, then our preaching is in vain and your faith is in vain" (1 Cor. 15:14).

Just as the person of Christ cannot be separated from the climax of his ministry on the cross, so also his death on the cross cannot be separated from his resurrection. If Jesus had died without rising from the dead, then his death would have been a pathetic defeat, but God did raise his son Jesus from the grave and gave to him a new resurrection life. Likewise the Christian believer not only dies to sin with

Christ, but also rises with Christ to new life. "Therefore, if anyone is in Christ, he is a new creation; the old has passed away, behold, the new has come" (2 Cor. 5:17).

Over the years various opponents of the Christian faith have realised that the resurrection is central to the whole Christian cause. They have therefore tried to disprove it and thus relegate Christianity to the dustbin of past history. Thus, for example, Frank Morison, the author of *Who Moved the Stone?*, set out to write a book which demonstrated that the resurrection was a mere myth. But the more he examined the evidence, the more he was convinced that Jesus did in fact rise from the dead. As a lawyer Prof. J. N. D. Anderson has also written to show that the evidence for the resurrection is sufficient for a legal case.

The Muslim already believes that God raised Jesus from this world, but in Islam Jesus probably never died and therefore was not raised from the dead. He was merely lifted to heaven like Enoch who "was not, for God took him" (Gen. 5:24) or Elijah who "went up by a whirlwind into heaven" (2 Kgs. 2:11). Islam therefore lacks the profoundly significant truth of the cross and resurrection together. The beauty of new life cannot be separated from the need of death to the old life and nature. So in Romans 6 Paul shows the symbolism of our baptism that we have "died to sin" because our "old self was crucified with him so that the sinful body might be destroyed and we might no longer be enslaved to sin" (v.6). But this death to sin leads immediately to the fact that "as Christ was raised from the dead by the glory of the Father, we too might walk in newness of life" (v.4).

What a glorious Saviour! And what a perfect salvation he has won for us! This is the heart of the good news which the apostles preached in the first century and it remains the high point of the Gospel for all men today. For Muslims also the Gospel should be marvellously good news. Let us pray that by the Holy Spirit we may be enabled to "make it clear, as I ought to speak" (Col. 4:4).

2 God

Although we have noted that the central features of the Gospel are the person of Jesus Christ and what he has done for us on the cross and in the resurrection, it remains obvious that these great truths depend on our beliefs concerning the character and nature of God himself. Over many centuries God patiently revealed to Israel his holy personality, his claims upon man and desires for us, his purposes of salvation and his steadfast covenant love. Only then did he climax this self-revelation through the person and work of his Son Jesus Christ. Here we face a double truth. We need a true background knowledge of the nature of God before we can adequately comprehend who Jesus is and what he has done for us. But likewise it remains true that Jesus Christ presents to us the perfect revelation of God. We can only come to the Father through Jesus Christ (John 14:6) and we can really only see and know God through seeing and knowing his Son (John 1:18; 12:45; 14:7, 9).

Many of the misunderstandings between Christians and Muslims stem from our fundamentally different concepts of the nature of God. As a foundation for the preaching of the person and work of Christ we shall need to teach the character of God as this is shown to us in the Bible. The glories of the Christian faith are based upon what we believe God is like. But we cannot communicate our idea of God to the Muslim unless we understand his own beliefs.

We may find the key to the Muslim's understanding of God in the very name "Allah". It would seem that this name stems from two Arabic roots: *al* and *ilah*.

(a) 'Al' – the one unique God

Al – 'the', the definite article – denotes that strong emphasis on the uniqueness of God. He brooks no rivals or equals. "There is no God but Allah." Although we have seen that this firm faith in the oneness of God may prove a real problem for the preaching of Jesus as the divine Son of God, yet we also noted that it presents difficulties for the Muslim with regard to the eternal nature and perfection of the Quran. The Christian on the other hand enjoys the truth that God is indeed one and yet at the same time his Word is eternally with him and in fact the Word actually is God (John 1:1, 2). Strict monotheism finds it very hard indeed to keep the glorious majesty and holiness of a God who is totally separate from his creation and yet at the same time make provision for God's gracious and loving presence with his people. Thus Islam has the twin doctrines of *tanzih*, separateness, and *mukhalafah*, otherness, which emphasise that God is a totally different entity from his creation and from men. He is therefore utterly removed from us.

Mohammed himself was able to keep this otherness of God in balance with the opposite truth that "God is nearer to us than our neck artery". Christian theology likewise maintains the twin emphases of God's transcendence and his immanence. This is made possible for us because God can on the one hand remain in all his splendid, majestic glory while on the other hand he becomes incarnate in the person of his Son, living alongside men as one of us. Islam allows no trinitarian theology with different persons in the one godhead, so it finds this balance almost impossible to maintain. Orthodox Muslims have largely lost sight of God's gracious immanence. God in his non-incarnated glory remains in the lofty splendour of his majesty.

(b) Ilah – God's power

Ilah comes from a root which means "to be strong". The great Islamicist Samuel Zwemer therefore states that "absolute sovereignty and ruthless omnipotence are his chief attributes", while Stanton corroborates this in his book *The Teaching of the Quran* where he says "the essence of Allah is power which overrides all his mere attributes and enables him to exercise them or not, as he pleases". Islam therefore stresses the power of God more than the holiness or love of God. In describing the attributes of God Islam and Christianity may agree and list the same characteristics, but they will place them in a different order. Both will describe God as all-powerful, all-merciful and all-holy. But while the Christian will insist that God's power is subject to his love and holiness, Islam will feel that God's love and holiness must never contradict his sovereign power.

The Christian therefore will happily use such expressions as "God must" and "God cannot", but the Muslim may describe these assertions as blasphemy. God cannot be limited. He is free and can exercise his power in whatever way he wishes. The Traditions of Islam even go so far as to put these words into God's mouth: "These to heaven and I care not; these to hell and I care not." In Islam God may do what he wishes. He may fortunately be merciful and holy and so act accordingly, but his sovereign free power allows him to do things which are contrary to his lesser attributes of mercy and holiness. It has been suggested that the God of Islam resembles a kind-hearted and good sheikh. He holds open court, in which his people may approach him with their requests. The sheikh has the power to dispense justice and benefits in accordance with whether he likes or dislikes the man before him. The sheikh's subject feels a certain degree of assurance in coming before him with his requests, because he knows that the sheikh is generally good and kind. But he can know no absolute assurance. So it is with the God of Islam.

The Christian however rejoices in a God whose very nature is love (1 John 4.8) and who *must* therefore love. The God of the Bible is also by nature holy (1 Pet. 1:15) and cannot be the author of evil or sin. God graciously limits his power in such a way that he *cannot* sin or act unlovingly. This allows the Christian to live in the assurance that God must keep his promises. This relates to every aspect of the Christian life. Otherwise prayer loses its significance; assurance of salvation becomes impossible and we can no longer trust confidently in the help and strength which God has promised us in our daily walk with him. We are not just splitting theological hairs when we affirm that God's power is subordinated to his love and holiness, whereas in Islam his power overrides his other attributes.

(c) Know God

In Islam God gave the Quran in order to reveal *his will* to man, but Islamic revelation does not aim to make *God* known to men. Christian concepts of revelation stand in distinct contrast to this. Jesus Christ as the living Word and the Bible as the written Word both have the overriding purpose of making God known to men. In each of the three great monotheistic religions (Judaism, Christianity and Islam) God's glorious holiness, power and majesty distance him from mere created beings. In each of these religions, mystics seek to overcome this by stressing intuitive, subjective experience of the presence of God. But there is a danger that they lack a true biblical revelation of the nature of God and that they also fail to have an adequate theological basis for spanning the huge gulf between God and man. Jewish Kabbalists, Muslim Sufis and Christian mystics can therefore easily play down the problem of sin which divides man from God. They may also fail to maintain the glory of God in his personal holiness.

It is true that more orthodox followers of the great monotheistic religions have much to learn from their mystical co-religionists. We can all fall into the trap of an arid theological truth with properly structured worship and prayer, but lack the warmth and beauty of intuitive and loving relationship with God. True Christian faith should bridge that gap. We have already noted the valiant efforts of Al-Ghazzali to relate a warm-hearted knowledge of God to the more orthodox and traditional faith of Islam, but generally Islam is still struggling with this dilemma. When the Christian presents the message of Jesus Christ in a Muslim context, he will want therefore to emphasise not only the theological truths of God's character but also the amazing fact that through Jesus Christ we can actually know God.

(i) We can know what God is like   The writer of the Epistle to the Hebrews declares that Jesus not only reflects the glory of God, but actually is "the very stamp of his nature" (Heb. 1:3). Likewise Paul affirms that Jesus came "in the form of God" (Phil. 2:6) and that he is "the image of God" (Col. 1:15). So John Owen in his commentary on Hebrews was able to state that "all the glorious perfections of the nature of God do belong unto and dwell in the person of the Son". Likewise Motyer in his *The Richness of Christ* says of Christ that he "possessed inwardly and displayed outwardly the divine attributes". Indeed, Jesus himself says "He who has seen me has seen the Father" (John 14:9). When we look at Jesus and come to know him, we see the very nature of God and know what God is like.

Just as the incarnate person of Jesus Christ reveals to us the nature of God, so also the Bible has as its primary aim the unveiling of God's person and character. As we read not only the descriptions of God but also the stories of his dealings with men, we come to an ever-growing understanding of what God is like.

(ii) We can know God   God does not desire merely that we should comprehend what he is like; he yearns for a personal relationship with us, in which he will be able to call us "his people" and we shall know him in a deeply personal way.

Muslims may often feel that God is so distant in his glorious power, that it is unthinkable that men should be able to relate to him in close personal knowledge. As Christians, we agree that without the mediating work of Christ it is indeed impossible for men to see or know God, but through and in Christ we are called to know God in such a way that we are united with him eternally.

(d) Sons of God

We noted earlier that God's purpose for men is that they should be in such intimate relationship with him that he can even call them his sons. Thus Adam in his perfect pre-Fall nature was the son of God (Luke 3:38). The Christian Gospel joyfully proclaims to fallen men the God-given possibility of being restored to that favoured position. If we believe in Jesus Christ and unite ourselves with him by faith, God promises to adopt us as his children. The apostle John states that "to all who received him, who believed in his name, he gave power to become children of God" (John 1:12). As we believe in Jesus Christ and receive him into the centre of our lives, God graciously makes it possible for us to become his children. So we can become by God's grace what Adam was in his original created nature.

The intimacy of this renewed relationship is boldly declared by Paul when he uses the term *Abba* for God the Father (Rom. 8:15; Gal. 4:6), the familiar word used by Jesus himself in his prayer to his Father in the Garden of Gethsemane (Mark 14:36).

After the fall of Adam and Eve God reminded Cain of the basic principle: "If you do well, will you not be accepted?" (Gen. 4:7). Sadly we know that neither Cain himself nor anyone since then could make himself adequately good in his character or in his actions to merit the favour and acceptance of the all-holy God. We can only be adopted as God's children on the basis of God's unmerited grace and love. The old A.V. translation of Ephesians 1:6 delightfully rejoiced that God has "made us accepted in the beloved". The translation hardly corresponds to the actual Greek text, but it reminds us that our acceptance as God's children does depend on God's grace and love which are shown to us "through Jesus Christ" (Eph. 1:5, 6). In the face of such undeserved love we can only respond with joyful gratitude. And in these days of growing personal and social insecurity, the Gospel of unmerited acceptance and love gives us a new sense of worth and a new freedom to love and to accept love.

The last paragraph reflects my own personal experience in my relationship with God. For several years I believed deeply in God and tried to follow him in ways that would please him. But I did not realise that my whole relationship with God depended not on what I was like or what I did for God, but rather on what God had graciously done for me in the cross and resurrection of Jesus Christ. When a fellow student at Oxford explained to me the marvel of grace through the work of Christ, this truth set me free to love and serve the Lord in deep gratitude.

Muslims all over the world are trying to serve God in humble obedience. In so doing they hope that at the final judgment God will reckon that their good works outweigh all their acts of disobedience to the revealed will of God. While admiring such loyal and dedicated service, the Christian will long to add the biblical teaching and experience of grace through the cross and resurrection of Jesus

Christ, leading to a joyful assurance of eternal life as a free gift from God.

3 Eternal life

For the Muslim, as indeed also for many biblically untaught Christians, our good and evil deeds in this life are kept in a great heavenly ledger awaiting the final day of reckoning. God's verdict will be pronounced upon us on that future day of judgment. And it is true that both the Quran and the Bible anticipate a final day of judgment, in which God will open the books and announce our eternal fate.

But the Bible also teaches that God's judgment is already active in this world. John's Gospel continually uses the present tense to describe the fact that we "have eternal life" or, on the other hand, that the "wrath of God abides on us" (John 3:36). This life cannot be compared to the years of study which lead up to a final examination, for we are already judged according to our works and according to our acceptance or rejection of Jesus Christ.

The Christian rejoices in the assurance of God's free gift to us of eternal life. We can look forward with confidence to the future judgment, because God has promised us salvation through Jesus Christ. The knowledge that all our works will be tested and sifted on that day makes us "take care" (1 Cor. 3:10) how we live and work, but we need not be afraid at all. For this reason the apostle John wrote his first epistle "that you may know that you have eternal life" (1 John 5:13) and thus reminds his readers of "the confidence which we have in him". Sadly this total assurance of the future eludes the Muslim. Islam forbids an assurance of salvation which is seen as presumption and as a denial of the sovereign freedom of God who could decide to condemn the believer to damnation. In the traditional list of the seventeen major sins[1] Islam includes "feeling safe from the wrath of God", but tempers this with another major sin which is "despairing of God's mercy". Thus, although he may not be wracked with doubt and despair, the Muslim can never rest in the joyful peace of knowing with absolute certainty that he has eternal life. The Quran qualifies the promise that "the blessed shall dwell in Paradise" with the further words "unless your Lord ordains otherwise" (Sura 11:108).

When working as an evangelist at a mission hospital in South Thailand I frequently watched Muslims approaching death. It was sad to see their fear. Would their good works be adequate to move God to show mercy? Would they remember the Creed in Arabic and be able to recite it perfectly to the angels of judgment in the grave? What joy for the Christian witness to be able to offer the Muslim the sure gift of eternal life if he puts his faith in Jesus Christ as Lord and Saviour!

(a) Heaven

We have noted the glories of the Christian message with regard to our privileged position that we know God and that we are adopted as his children. These two great truths relate closely to the further fact of eternal life. We have been adopted into the very family of God and this new

---

[1] The seventeen major sins are *kufr* (idolatrous infidelity), constant minor sins, despairing of God's mercy, feeling safe from God's wrath, false witness, falsely accusing a Muslim of adultery, false oaths, magic, drinking alcohol, taking an orphan's property, usury, adultery, unnatural sin, theft, murder, fleeing in battle against infidels and disobedience to parents.

family relationship abides through all eternity. Just as we shall always be the children of our earthly parents, so our oneness with God as his children stretches before us through all the trials of this life and on into eternal ages beyond. As Paul rightly declares with triumph, nothing can separate us from the love of God in Christ Jesus our Lord (Rom. 8:39).

What is our picture of heaven? Do our minds conjure up an image of worldly pleasures? Both Christians and Muslims have been tempted to fall into this error. Or do we have a more escapist and negative picture, in which we are freed from the sins, griefs and pains of this world? Again, we find this aspect of the future in both religions. And surely both are to some extent true. Heaven will certainly outdo all the joys and pleasures possible in this life. When our children have asked us whether their favourite teddy or other toy will also be there in heaven, we have sometimes assured them that in heaven they will have everything they could possibly desire and still more. Likewise in heaven we shall certainly weep no more tears, our frail bodies will be transformed and all sickness and suffering will be left behind.

But surely heaven is more than all this. The central feature of eternal life in heaven consists of our oneness with God. When a young couple fall in love, it is bliss just to be together. The ecstasy of heaven also consists of unhindered oneness with the Lord whom we love and who loves us. As his children we shall enjoy him for ever and we shall bask in the warmth of his deep love. As Jesus himself said, "This is eternal life, that they know thee the only true God, and Jesus Christ" (John 17:3).

Such a concept of eternal life will not be totally alien to the Muslim mind, but it will certainly add a new dimension of glory to even the highest Islamic ideas of eternal life. And for most Muslims the Christian view of heaven will

shine with incomparable brightness in vivid contrast to
their normally rather materialistic idea.

(b) Sin forgiven

In talking of eternal life, knowing God and being his
adopted children, we have again and again mentioned that
these wonderful gifts of God come to us through the work
of Christ on the cross. The New Testament has a variety of
deeply significant terms to describe what Christ has done
for us by his death on the cross – redemption, reconcilia-
tion, atonement, justification, propitiation. By his death
Jesus has saved us from our sins and from the power of the
evil one. Our sin, which once separated us from God, has
been covered and forgiven so perfectly that God does not
even remember it any more.

The Muslim hopes God will overlook his sins because his
good works outweigh his evil deeds. Islam has adopted the
Zoroastrian belief that our sins and good works will be
weighed in heavenly balances at the judgment. When I was
in Singapore we displayed a poster showing a set of scales.
The balance was tipped down by a heavy weight of sins,
while the good works were very light. Beneath the picture
was the Bible verse: 'You are weighed in the balances and
found wanting" (Dan. 5:27). This poster caused minor riots
and public disturbances. Its message touched a raw nerve.

Islam lacks any theory of atonement and therefore finds
it hard to reconcile merciful forgiveness with the holiness of
God. Inevitably therefore Islam is somewhat weak in its
teaching on forgiveness. The apostle Paul struggled with
this problem too – how can God remain utterly holy and
just, but at the same time forgive those sins which in all
justice ought to be judged? In Romans 3 he sees the
solution to this problem in the atoning work of Christ on the
cross. God has himself sent his Son to pay the penalty for
our sin. God in his holiness does judge sin, but takes the

whole weight of our guilt and condemnation upon himself in the person of his Son. He can therefore forgive our sin while at the same time exercising his justice in righteous judgment upon the sin of the world.

By faith we align ourselves with Christ, dying with him and rising with him to new life. By faith we accept what he has done for us on the cross. By the grace of God in Christ our sins are forgiven and we are saved. This message contrasts with the teachings of Islam in at least two significant ways.

(i) God loves sinners Before the time of Jesus many Jews held that the kingdom of God belongs to the righteous and the pious, but Jesus turned this teaching on its head. He demonstrated in his life and taught by his words that God's gifts are made available to all sinners who will recognise their sin and turn in repentance and faith to follow Jesus. Jesus did not come to earth for the sake of the righteous, but to save sinners. Closely parallel to such traditional Jewish thought, Islam believes that God's favour rests on those who submit themselves to the will of God. The Gospel of God's loving invitation to sinners to feast at his banquet of forgiveness offers unexpected relief to the Muslim of tender conscience.

(ii) It's never too late! Islam offers little hope to the man who has spent his life in sin and disobedience. Only judgment awaits such people. As life proceeds, the weight of our sins increases day by day and moment by moment. And if we are already old, we may lack time and opportunity to accumulate adequate good works to counterbalance our sins.

To such a person the Christian Gospel offers hope. If he will receive God's offer of forgiveness and new life through Christ, his old nature with all its sin is put to death with Christ on the cross and he will rise to a new life with a new nature in Christ. The New Testament gives a beautiful example of this in Jesus' words to the thief on the cross next to his own. Jesus promised this man that despite a life spent in crime "today you will be with me in Paradise" (Luke 23:43). The thief was soon to die and would have no opportunity to demonstrate his repentance by a life of good works. He would never be able to perform good works whose merit would outweigh his life of disobedience to God's commands. But still Christ's promise comes to him – and to all who repent and put their faith in Christ.

When I worked as a missionary among Muslims, several men read this story in Luke's Gospel and objected that it was unjust. We discussed together the whole issue of death-bed conversion. They could not understand that the redeeming work of Christ on the cross did actually make such conversions just. From man's point of view we are never adequately good to merit eternal life and it might therefore be said that the salvation of men is never just. But from God's point of view his justice is vindicated by the fact of the cross.

While some Muslims may object to the idea of death-bed conversions, to others God's love for sinners comes as a message of hope like cool water in a desert. For sinners Islam is an arid desert, into which the Gospel comes with fresh hope.

4 The Holy Spirit
Without the reality of the Christian doctrine of the Trinity the whole message of the Gospel will founder. We rejoice in the nature of God the Father. We base our faith on the fact that God did not remain in glorious majesty utterly apart from the world and from us as mortals. He came to us in the person of his Son, Jesus Christ, lived with us, died for us, rose again in victory over death and ascended to the Father – and we with him die to our old sinful nature, rise to new life and ascend with him so that we can say that we sit

with him in heavenly places (Eph. 2:6). But Jesus has now risen from this earth and his disciples feared that they would be left alone. God the Father and God the Son reside in glory, but we men must for a while remain on earth in imperfection. God in his three-fold nature meets our need. He sends us his Holy Spirit to be with us and in us. Through the Holy Spirit the presence of God never leaves us.

The Christian church has sadly not kept up to date in its formulations of the doctrine of the Trinity. We still use ancient Greek creeds with vocabulary and philosophical thought-forms unrelated to our present society, so most ordinary Christians never really grasp the wonder of God's Trinitarian nature. As a result we are often defensive and threatened when we come face to face with non-Trinitarian monotheistic systems like Islam, Judaism or the Jehovah's Witnesses.

Having looked a little at the Father and the Son in previous pages, let us now turn our attention to the significance of the Holy Spirit in our witness to Muslims.

We know from the New Testament that the Holy Spirit is called the Spirit of life and it is He who imparts life to believers in Jesus Christ. He then fills them, empowers them and sends them out in active mission. But in this section we shall note some other results of the Spirit's work in us.

(a) Growth

In the Old Testament the Spirit of God sometimes came upon key charismatic leaders of Israel and they were temporarily filled with the Spirit, but in the New Testament Christians experienced the permanent presence of the indwelling Holy Spirit. The Christian therefore never struggles alone in his battles against sin, temptation and the Devil. By his Spirit, God himself works in and for us. Both Islam and Christianity observe the reality of this constant internal warfare, but their basic approach differs radically. In Islam man is held responsible for the outcome of the battle, although it is allowed that God in his great mercy may help his followers. In Judaism likewise each individual is personally responsible for ensuring that the good spirit overcomes the evil spirit. But in the Christian faith it is God himself who fights the battle against Satan and we merely act as his accomplices in cooperation with him. It is God who by his Spirit works in us (Phil. 2:13) and we can therefore look forward with confidence to a future of ever-increasing victory (Phil. 1:6).

In the New Testament the Christian life is seen as one of constant growth and development. Like a small seed which grows into a large tree or like leaven which gradually permeates the whole lump of dough, the presence of God's Holy Spirit in us increasingly affects every area of our lives. As a baby must grow into full maturity, so new birth in Christ initiates us into a life of growth. As we progress through life, the Spirit adds to us new areas of love and holiness. Even the perfect Jesus "grew" (Luke 2:40) and "increased in wisdom and in stature, and in favour with God and man" (Luke 2:52).

As Christians we should be deeply aware of our sinful failure to live up to the standards we set for ourselves, let alone the perfect standards of the all-holy God. We long for lives which are more closely attuned to the pattern of the life of Jesus. We note with abhorrence how often sin assails us, we hurt other people and cause distress to the Lord we love. But what an encouragement and reassurance to know that the Holy Spirit in us is changing us!

Islam believes in a God who helps men in particular situations, but it seems to have little stress on God's work in changing the very nature of man from within or therefore of growth in spirituality, holiness and love.

(b) Spirit of love

Islam has never paralleled the supreme emphasis which Christian teaching gives to love. Jesus said that the whole Law could be summarised in the one word "love" – love for God and for our neighbour. He stressed to his disciples the importance of his new commandment to them to love one another. John, who was so personally intimate with his master, likewise became known as the "apostle of love" because of the centrality of love in all his teaching. And Paul too places love first in his list of the fruit of the Spirit (Gal. 5:22). In the midst of his specific teaching on the gifts of the Spirit he devotes an entire and often-quoted chapter to love. The gifts of tongues, prophecy, discernment, knowledge, mountain-moving faith or even martyrdom remain empty and useless unless founded on love (1 Cor. 13.1–3).

Islam stresses obedience, submission and strict subservience to God's revealed will. Love needs to be demonstrated as well as preached if we are to prove that the message of Jesus Christ is indeed "good news".

(i) *Love for God*   All too often the Christian faith has been confused with a Western Protestant work ethic together with an undue emphasis on efficiency and punctuality to the neglect of less pragmatic virtues. Whereas the Hindu or Buddhist image of holiness means quiet prayer and meditation, the Christian leader is noted for his businesslike efficiency as he rushes from meeting to meeting. Mohammed himself was evidently much impressed by the Christian monks of his time who endured lives of solitary prayer in the desert regions. It is true that he particularly noted their fear of God (*rahib*, the Arabic term for a monk, stems from a root meaning "to fear"), but he must also have observed the intense prayer which lay at the heart of their devotion to God. Sadly, however, there is no evidence at all that Mohammed saw love in their lives.

Although there have been some Muslims who have
developed a moving experience of love for God, generally
speaking one has to say that the idea remains foreign to
most Muslims. As Christians we need to ask the Holy Spirit
to fill us with a new and ever-growing love for the Lord –
and this should not just be in order to impress Muslims, but
genuinely for our own sake and because such love pleases
God. But it is true that evident love for the Lord will attract
the more spiritually minded Muslim. In witness with Muslims we cannot afford mere theological discussion which
remains cool and objective; the Muslim must be able to see
a heart that burns with warm love for God.

It is the work of the Holy Spirit to foster within us such a
deep love for God that we long to please him. The Christian serves and obeys God because he loves him and desires
to express his gratitude, not because of any legalism which
seeks to earn God's favour. The Spirit also gives us his
power to enable us to please God.

(ii) Love for the brethren   We have already noted the strong
emphasis in Islam on the *umma*, the Muslim community.
The character of the *umma* reflects down from the totality
of the Muslim community worldwide to such smaller units
as the clan or the family. Islam evokes a great sense of
loyalty in the cohesive unity of the *umma*, but again there is
little if any idea of real love.

Living in the deeply caring community of the Christian
college where I teach, and constantly meeting Christians all
over the world in my wider preaching and teaching ministry, I particularly rejoice in the beauty of God's great gift of
love between Christians. If a Muslim can experience for
himself the reality of such love and feel the atmosphere of
such a Christian fellowship, he will be intensely impressed.

Sadly, we all fail to live out the perfection of loving
fellowship which God purposes for his children. And many
churches tragically lack any evidence of such love. In more

recent years, however, there has been a renewed emphasis on the fact that Christians form a united body together and that loving fellowship is of primary importance as a key characteristic of the Christian Church. For witness among Muslims this love must be seen not only between individual Christians within any one church or fellowship, but must also be evident between different churches.

(iii) Love for others As Christians we have been excited by the fact that God himself loved us when we were still "dead through our trespasses" (Eph. 2:4, 5). His love is no mere response to our faith, but rather God takes the initiative in loving us while we are still outside his kingdom. We love him because he first loved us (1 John 4:19). God's love reaches out to embrace the whole world (John 3:16).

Similarly as Christians our love should extend beyond the confines of the Christian Church to care for the world outside. Many Muslim converts to Christ will testify that they were attracted by the fact that certain Christians really did love them. In every aspect of our Christian living we are to demonstrate love for the world. The non-Christian visitor to our church services should be able to sense a truly caring concern and thus feel at home. In our active evangelism we should not only confront Muslims with the Gospel of Christ, but also woo them in love. This will require a genuine sensitivity. In our ordinary lives in our homes and at work we should so love people that they feel a warm personal approach in us. As Christians we should be in the forefront of all activities aimed at meeting the personal and social needs of men and women.

(c) Spirit of truth

To the Muslim, religion forms an integral part of everyday life and normally he will enter freely into religious and theological debate. He has no thought that such questions are a private matter between himself and his God. The

Christian witness will therefore find little difficulty in entering into such discussion with his Muslim friend. Unfortunately such talk often degenerates into fierce argument with both sides heatedly defending their faith. In such an atmosphere truth slips easily away and is replaced by propaganda.

The Christian needs constantly to remember that the Holy Spirit is the Spirit of truth, and Jesus himself claimed to be the truth. It behoves us as disciples of Jesus to stick close to truth and not attempt to promote the honour of our Lord by means of semi-truths. We shall eschew all temptations to score debating points rather than lovingly and patiently unfolding the truth.

We have all heard sermons which make the Christian life sound idyllic. "Come to Christ and he will give you . . .", but they fail to mention that we are not suddenly transported into perfection. We grow gradually in God's gifts and graces through hard struggles and battles. The Christian life contains tremendous blessings, but it is not all sweetness and light. The Muslim will see through propagandist preaching which is not really honest, but will be more attracted by a true explanation of the realities of Christian discipleship.

A friend told me recently about a Christian who preached on how God answers prayer. He told story after story of remarkable and miraculous answers to prayer, urging and encouraging his listeners to trust the Lord and pray with faith. My friend commented that in fact there were long periods of several years' duration between the events recounted in the preacher's stories. With a wry smile he commented that perhaps his friend only prayed once every few years! Or did the preacher experience times when God did not apparently answer his prayers in such signal fashion? He made prayer sound so easy and automatic, whereas we know that God is no genie of the lamp who jumps out to do our bidding every time we rub him in prayer.

Likewise a Muslim will sense the propagandism of the shaving-soap-advertisement testimony, in which the Christian describes the horrors of his pre-Christian life just as the advertisement portrays the rough unshaven face under the title "before". The advertisement then shows the same face smothered in thick lather, leading on to the final picture of a sexily smooth and velvet skin with the heading "after". The Christian's testimony may parallel this unduly simplistic approach by contrasting the victorious Christian life with the hopelessness of his previous existence. The "lather" of the blood of Christ does indeed produce the miracle of a new life, but the Spirit of truth should move us to complete and open honesty.

We may well find that Muslims will at first fail to match our willingness to share and confess failures and difficulties, but finally truth must prevail if anyone is to come into a genuine relationship with the Christ who is the truth.

5 Christian marriage

Although marriage as an institution is under grave threat in many areas of Western society, the Christian ideal shines like a beacon in the darkness. The witness of the Christian Church here in Britain will stand or fall according to whether we maintain loving, godly Christian homes. In working among Muslims my wife and I have found that many people have first been attracted to the Christian faith through the witness of the home. True unity of spirit acts like a magnet. People see the reality of a couple who lovingly admire one another. They sense the confidence and peace which love inspires.

Much has been written in recent years about the role of women in Muslim society. In our experience among Muslims in various countries we rarely encountered a married couple who shared deeply in love. Many wives envied my wife's absolute confidence that her husband would not prove unfaithful and that she would never have to face the trauma of being divorced. Such assurance is sadly lacking in the hearts of so many Muslim women.

Conclusion

The "good news" is glorious! Our hearts and minds thrill in a fresh way when we observe the beauty of Jesus Christ in comparison with the life and faith of Islam. In the power of the Holy Spirit it *is* possible to share Christian truths with Muslims, and to show them how to enjoy the same fullness of salvation which we have experienced in Christ.

With such a longing in our hearts, we inevitably ask ourselves, "How am I to witness?"

6
How to Witness

Facing the difficult task of mission among Muslims, Christians have attempted to use a variety of approaches. It is not easy to measure the relative effectiveness of the various methods, for in the heartlands of Islam no form of Christian witness seems to evoke much definite response. However, Vander Werff in his excellent study of mission methods in witness to Muslims does give some interesting insights from the history of Christian missions in several countries.

As both Christians and Muslims believe in revelation through a book, the use of literature has obviously played a considerable part in Christian mission among Muslims. Some have scattered portions of the Bible and other literature widely throughout the local population in the hope that this will lead to a general interest in the Gospel and to the actual conversion of a few individuals. Others have rather preferred to restrict their distribution of Christian literature to a few people whom they know personally and with whom they can study and discuss the contents. Books have been written and many stories can be told of leading Christians who were convinced of the truth of Jesus Christ through reading Christian literature.

Christian missions have pioneered medical and educational work in many countries throughout the world. Such institutions have not only aimed at the preaching of the Gospel, but have also been true expressions of Christian love. In recent years they have come under considerable attack for being mere underhand subterfuges for evangelism, but these attacks are not generally fair. It needs also to be said that many Muslim countries will not permit any form of direct evangelism and so the Christian Church is restricted to this form of mission. But it is true that through such indirect means people can see the outworkings of the Christian faith, ask questions when curiosity or spiritual hunger is aroused and thus come to understand who Jesus is and what he has done.

While Islam has largely spread in Africa and Asia through traders and other "non-professional" missionaries, Christianity in the past has relied unduly on paid professionals to preach the Gospel in other lands. This trend is being reversed today and we are seeing a growing number of Christians going overseas in their secular callings, but with a definite missionary purpose. In many Muslim countries this is the only way to obtain entry visas and thus gain any possibility of sharing the good news of Jesus Christ. Such workers will need very real maturity, wisdom and sensitivity as they live out their Christian faith with little opportunity of fellowship or spiritual support. But their quiet testimony of life plus the occasional word of witness can demonstrate to the Muslim population that Christians are not as bad as they may have thought. Over the years through prolonged contact with people they may stimulate some friends to desire a more satisfying faith than they are experiencing in Islam. Unfortunately many Christians working in Muslim countries lack adequate knowledge both of Islam and of their own faith to be able to communicate effectively. And some even lack the spiritual motivation, believing that all religions are of equal validity and therefore there is no need for a Muslim to know Jesus Christ as Lord and Saviour.

The Christian worker in the heartland countries of Islam faces great opportunities not only directly with Muslims, but also in helping and teaching the other expatriate Christians there from Pakistan, Egypt or European nations. The well-instructed Christian may be able to help these other Christians to share their faith wisely but relevantly with their Muslim fellow-workers. Christians who are going to work in Muslim countries need to get some training beforehand in biblical and theological studies as well as in communication of the Christian faith in a Muslim context.

Christian girls should go to traditional Muslim countries only if they are willing to adapt to a culture where women are by no means equal to men. Similarly, married couples will experience real difficulties in Muslim lands if the wife wears the trousers.

1 What can I do?

Again and again young Christians ask me this question – what can I do? They have been challenged by Christian talks concerning the large number of Muslims living and studying in their midst. They know that they ought to be witnessing to this apparently solid phalanx of the followers of Islam. But how?

(a) Get to know them

There can be no possibility of witness as long as we all remain within our narrow circles without really meeting with others. The first stage in witness is therefore to get to know Muslims. Every opportunity should be taken to talk and share with them. This may come about through studying together or helping them with their studies. It may come through sharing together in everyday activities like shopping, work or sport. If we long to bring the message of Jesus Christ to our Muslim neighbours, we shall look for any such possibility to make personal contact with them. Those who seek will find. Those who sit around bemoaning the difficulty of making friends with Muslims will not succeed.

In getting to know Muslims, we shall of course learn increasingly about their culture, their way of thinking and their religion. If we ask friendly questions, they will be delighted to share with us about their faith and their way of life. Learning through such conversations will be further helped by more reading, or embarking on a short study course in Islam.

(b) Love your neighbour

People quickly sense whether we really love them. They know if we merely desire to convert them without any deep concern for them as people. Perhaps our greatest need is to pray that the Holy Spirit will give us his gift of love for our Muslim neighbours. Love will always find a way to express itself. Real love is wonderfully attractive and the Muslim will be touched by it.

Christian love will be expressed in generous hospitality. The New Testament emphasises that hospitality is a mark of Christian spirituality (Rom. 12:13; 1 Tim. 3:2; Titus 1:8; 1 Pet. 4:9). In most Muslim-influenced cultures, too, hospitality is of supreme importance and stands as an essential cardinal virtue. If the witness of the Christian is to attract, it must be expressed in connection with open-hearted hospitality. The Christian student should be quick to invite Muslim fellow students to coffee or to meals in his room. The Christian home should be open to Muslim neighbours. Visiting and being visited is the sure way to friendship and thus also to the opportunity to share faith.

In a loving relationship with Muslims it is crucial to learn their customs. Cultural sensitivity is a sign of genuine love. Paul made himself a Jew to the Jews and a Greek to the Greeks. His example should be followed as far as possible. This is particularly important in questions of food. Pork and other food derived from the pig will obviously be avoided. I was impressed to hear recently how the Christian community in West Sumatra has now stopped eating anything associated with the pig. They live in a strongly Muslim area and rightly feel that pork will cut them off from the Muslim population. Likewise, alcoholic drinks are offensive to the Muslim.

In the New Testament loving and giving go together (e.g. John 3:16). Both immigrant communities and also foreign students present us with enormous challenges. They face great problems in adjusting to life in our country. Let us look out for the chance to encourage, welcome and help them.

(c) Invite them to church

When a Muslim begins to relax with us and feel at ease, he may well be interested to see what goes on in a Christian church or meeting. Even a Christian Union prayer meeting may be spiritually stimulating for him as he will not have heard Christians pray before. Of course it is important to be careful that the church or meeting is suitable for a totally non-Christian Muslim. For example, we must not invite Muslims to churches which have offensive forms. Anything which looks at all like an idol will put them off the Christian faith. Bowing to a cross at the front of the church will appear to them idolatrous.

Churches and Christian Unions may like to take the initiative in inviting Muslims to speak to their members about Islam. Many Muslims would be honoured and glad to share their faith with us. Likewise people from overseas could be invited to talk about their country. This will promote understanding of the overseas situation and lead to more effective prayer for missionaries and for the Church. If the Muslim comes to the church not as a vulnerable nonentity but as the honoured speaker, he will feel far less threatened as he ventures into a new and foreign environment.

(d) Personal testimony

Few ordinary Christians will gain a deep knowledge of Islam and Muslim culture and theology. Intimate understanding will inevitably remain the preserve of the specialist. But all of us can grow in knowledge. Meanwhile we want to be able to share our faith in Christ and our experience of his salvation.

Various little books have been written which give a simple method of approach to evangelism among Muslims. Since the realities and complexities of actual encounter with living Muslims do not allow for any neat pre-packed evangelism, few of us will be in a position to engage in a witness closely related to Muslim backgrounds. But all of us can share what Jesus Christ means to us with joy and enthusiasm. However, as soon as we open our mouths in witness to God's grace in Christ, we shall inevitably stimulate questions concerning the Trinity, the Son of God, revelation in the Bible, the meaning of salvation and a multitude of other serious issues. Witness to Muslims forces us to go deeper in our own study of the Christian faith. While we may sometimes confess that we do not know all the theological answers or understand the deep mysteries of the Christian faith, our joyful testimony to what God has done for us in Christ and by his Spirit will remain real and attractive.

In sharing our experience of Christ it may prove helpful to ask the Muslim about his faith. We might well exchange views on what prayer means to us. Or it might be good to share together our feelings about death and the judgment. Discussion of such topics will prove both interesting and instructive.

In witness among Muslims there is one thing which needs to be avoided at all costs. We have mentioned it before, but it is worth repeating. Heated theological argument never helps. It drives a man into the shell of his convictions. I have noticed often that quite nominal and irreligious Muslims can become fanatical advocates of their faith when pushed into a theological argument. In this way we merely strengthen the hold of Islam. Such an unloving atmosphere also fails to demonstrate the gracious love which should characterise the follower of Christ. And in such a confrontation neither the Muslim nor the Christian will be able to share honestly and openly, so our witness will lack the winsome wooing of love.

(e) Literature

We have already mentioned the use of Christian literature in mission among Muslims, but I would wish to underline the role that this plays.

The Bible has a totally different character from the Quran or other Islamic writings. Its obvious God-centred spirituality and its striking relevance to daily life cannot but make a deep impression on anyone who has never read it at all before. Despite the theological problems concerning the doctrine of revelation, it will be most helpful if the Muslim can be encouraged to read the Bible for himself.

I have often told Muslims that I have read their Quran, so why should they not read our Bible? If they are afraid to do so, I have sometimes asked whether they are afraid to search honestly for truth. In Asia I used a form of picture language, saying that anyone who has Thai rice will not be attracted away to inferior breeds of rice. As a Christian I have confidence in the message of Jesus Christ and am therefore free to examine all other religions without anxiety. Does the Muslim not have the same freedom? If not, why not?

The Bible is a very big book and few will want to read the whole of it at first. Where should the Muslim begin? I have often recommended Genesis and Proverbs. They give a good religious background which will form a foundation for the full message of the New Testament. Culturally they are written in a style which fits the Muslim reader generally. And these two Old Testament books do not give rise to very much disagreement or controversy. If the Muslim enjoys these books, then I suggest he continue with a Gospel (preferably Luke) and then the book of Acts.

But we may well want to sell, lend or distribute not only the Bible itself, but also other Christian books. Christian biographies can be particularly helpful.

(f) Prayer

The orthodox Muslim places great emphasis on the importance of the prayer times. If he is strict in his religion, he will put other things aside at the prayer times in order to pray. It is therefore vital that he realises that the Christian also believes in and practises prayer. In some cases it may even be helpful if we can join him in prayer, so that he actually hears the Christian communing with God through Jesus Christ.

But prayer must not be merely in order to impress Muslims with our relationship with God through Jesus Christ. As Christians we do believe that God answers prayer. Prayer must play a significant part in our evangelistic strategy. We are called to continue steadfastly in prayer (Col. 4:2) and to pray with such faith that even the mountains of Islam are moved (Matt. 17:20). In prayer we are engaging in a spiritual warfare against the forces of darkness to cooperate with God in the unleashing of the redemptive power of the Holy Spirit. In answer to prayer God will graciously work to reveal himself to our Muslim friends.

2 Dialogue or proclamation?

In more recent years many Christians have emphasised the role of dialogue in Christian witness. This has been particularly true of more liberal Christians, but evangelicals have followed in their footsteps with a new emphasis on dialogue but with a more biblical understanding of the word. In all

Christian circles we are having to ask serious questions concerning the nature of mission in modern multi-racial society where the different religions rub shoulders together and must therefore determine their relationship one to the other. As Max Warren said some years ago, "The Christian Church has not yet seriously faced the theological problem of 'coexistence' with other faiths." He then asked the fundamental question whether the Gospel of Christ has universal validity or whether it is merely for peoples of Christian background. Our understanding of dialogue will depend on our answer to this sort of question.

The word "dialogue" is used in two different ways. It is important that we do not confuse the two and thus cloud the debate about the validity of dialogue in Christian mission.

(a) Not monologue

Few Christians today would query the fact that we need to listen carefully to those of other faiths and hear what they say as well as demanding that they listen to us. In *Sandals at the Mosque* Cragg talks of dialogue as reverent, tactful, tender and sensitive. John Stott in *Christian Mission in the Modern World* quotes J. G. Davies' *Dialogue with the World* in saying that "monologue is entirely lacking in humility". Certainly as one studies the history of Christian mission from the time of the apostles through to Carey and the early Protestant pioneers, most of the key men listened keenly to the people among whom they worked. Carey himself spent much time and labour in translating Hindu classics into English and teaching new missionaries the philosophical thought-forms of Hinduism. Indeed, his home mission board rebuked him for thus concentrating on heathenism rather than simply preaching the Gospel! One hopes that today's missionaries will not be fit objects for E. M. Forster's biting words: "poor little talkative Christianity".

(b) All roads lead to Rome

The Anglican Congress at Keele defined dialogue in terms
of listening and learning as well as speaking and instructing.
It is certainly true that as Christians we have much to learn
personally from Muslims, as indeed from people of all
backgrounds. We are constantly rebuked by their dedicated piety, for example. But this does not mean that Islam
can add truth to an otherwise deficient Christian revelation.
While Cromwell's plea "For God's sake, I pray you,
bethink you, you may be mistaken," surely reminds us that
our understanding of the Christian faith may always be
inadequate or even actually incorrect, nevertheless the
Christian would not accept that God's revelation in the
incarnate Word and in the written Word needs correction
at the hands of Islam.

But many theologians today are saying that all revelations are mere human gropings after ultimate truth. The
Bible, the Quran, the Vedas and other religious books
contain only partial truth distorted by their human authors,
they say. Thus John Hick in his *Truth and Dialogue* claims
that all religions and their inspired books are merely developments of and expressions of "the same ultimate divine
reality" and dialogue aims at learning from others in order
to attain a fuller grasp of truth in which "our present
conflicting doctrines will be transcended". In his view,
then, all religions lead towards the same goal and we shall
have much to learn from one another. We see how closely
this resembles the earlier syncretistic movements which
aimed to fuse all religions through taking the best from
each.

(c) Christian presence

The practice of dialogue often goes hand in hand with the
theory that Christ is already present in other faiths and the
task of mission is therefore just to unfold the beauties of

Christ in Islam which will find their final flowering in the fullness of Christ in the Christian revelation. It is said therefore that the aim of dialogue is "to meet Christ in the other person". As we listen, we shall learn of the Christ already present in the Muslim.

The concept of Christian presence is a reaction against callous dismissal of non-Christians to hell. Theologians of this persuasion ask whether a God of loving mercy could condemn the majority of mankind to such a fate. They also note elements of truth and beauty in other faiths and their adherents, affirming that Christ is God's agent in bringing good into the world. As Tolstoy said, "Where love is, God is". Evangelical Christians will want to restate our re-formed biblical teaching on the origin of good in non-Christian man. The image of God in which we were created remains in us. God also works through general revelation.

We notice that talk of dialogue comes almost exclusively from Christians rather than from Muslims, although there are some Muslims who are willing to share in discussions with Christians. But generally the Muslim will reject the basic principles of dialogue. He does not agree that Christ is present in Islam nor that Islam and Christianity are both partial truths. The Muslim is confident that he has a message from God which he must deliver to those who have not yet submitted to the will of God. Many Christians have been somewhat embarrassed in dialogues with Muslims, because they find that their Muslim friends are confident of their faith while the Christians are only willing to speak tentatively.

(d) Dialogue in the New Testament
In the welter of debate about dialogue we need to look more carefully at the New Testament and see how the word is used there. In this way we may gain some biblical insight into mission principles.

The New Testament uses three Greek words which contain the root from which we get our English word "dialogue". Significantly Luke uses two of these in his Gospel, but then changes to the third word in the Acts of the Apostles. The words used in the Gospel always imply considerable questioning and uncertainty of thought. This also coincides with the use of these words in Matthew and Mark. Thus when the angel Gabriel came to Mary in Luke 1:29 she was "greatly troubled at the saying and dialogued in her mind what sort of greeting this might be". So also in Luke 3:15 "all men dialogued in their hearts concerning John, whether perhaps he were the Christ." Throughout his Gospel Luke uses these words to denote real uncertainty (cf. Luke 5:21, 22; 6:8; 9:46, 47; 12:17; 20:14; 24:38). Paul uses these same words with a negative sense of uncertain questioning which he sees as an expression of empty futility (Rom. 1:21; 14:1; 1 Cor. 3:20; Phil. 2:14; 1 Tim. 2:8) and James 2:4 also calls these dialoguings "evil".

The Book of Acts presents us with a marked contrast, using a different word for "dialogue". Now Luke avoids any suggestion that the apostles were wracked with uncertainty or questionings as they engaged in mission. Thus in Acts 17:2, 17 the Revised Standard Version rightly translates it as "argued". The word has the context of proclaiming (17:3) and evangelising (17:18) with definite and positive preaching. Throughout the Book of Acts Luke uses the word "dialogue" with this sense of convinced preaching, but the apostolic proclamation is often dialogue in the sense that it is not mere monologue. Thus the dialoguing in Acts 24:25 is clearly in the context of debate with Felix.

What then may we learn from the biblical evidence which may guide us in our mission to Muslims? Like the apostles, we shall want to aim to convince the Muslim of the truth of the Christian message, for we shall preach it with assurance. Our aim will be that the Muslim should be converted to faith in Jesus Christ. Bishop John Taylor in his *Face to Face* has said, "We must covet for all men what, in our moments of highest aspiration, we covet for ourselves, the privileges of walking consciously in the steps and in the power of the Crucified. For in a universe of which he is the Maker and the Lord, the fullness of life cannot mean less than that." But we shall want to engage in evangelistic mission in such a way that we can listen to the heartfelt needs and deepest thoughts of our Muslim friends. Such an approach to dialogue will also be respected by the convinced Muslim, while he may well despise the lack of sure faith implied by a form of dialogue which does not seek to convince and convert him.

3 Through existing churches

The apostle Paul burned with passionate longing for the salvation of his own people, the Jews. He testified that he had "great sorrow and unceasing anguish in his heart" (Rom. 9:2) and that it was his "heart's desire and prayer to God" for them that they might put their faith in Jesus Christ and thus be saved (Rom. 10:1). How then could he justify the fact that he dedicated his life to mission among Gentiles? In Rom. 11:13, 14 he gives an answer. He rejoices in his ministry among the Gentiles because through it he aims to "make my fellow Jews jealous, and thus save some of them".

Despite the fact that the early Church consisted entirely of Jewish believers, it still remained true that the great majority of Jews resisted the claims of Jesus to be the Messiah. In contrast to the relative hardness of Jews, many Gentiles hungered for a more satisfying faith than their traditional religions and received the Gospel with open hearts (e.g. Acts 13:48). Paul understood that the divine strategy for mission to the Jews required him to concentrate

his energies on reaching the Gentiles in order that Jews
might in their turn be attracted to Christ through their
Gentile Christian neighbours.

How does this relate to our mission among Muslims?
Clearly the bulk of Muslims parallel the first-century Jews
in their firm resistance to the Gospel of Jesus Christ. Should
we concentrate our attention on other peoples who are not
Muslim and may be won more easily for Christ? For
example, in Sudan should we temporarily forsake the Arab
Muslim population while we establish and build up churches among the African peoples of that country in the hope
that the Muslims may see the beauty of Christ in the
churches of other races? The same question could be raised
for the strategy of mission in many West African countries,
as also in Malaysia and Indonesia. Likewise, should we
attempt to evangelise Muslims in Britain through the life of
white British churches? No easy or glib answer will prove
satisfactory. On the one hand it has to be said that sadly
such Gospel witness is often hampered by bitter racialism.
Arabs may even find it easier to receive the Gospel from a
European than from an African; Malays may resist a
Gospel dressed in Chinese forms. And the churches may
retain such antipathy towards the Muslim races that they
will not receive a convert or enquirer from among them. On
the other hand foreign missionaries from overseas never
present a very adequate image of the Christian faith because of race, language and culture. And the witness of
foreign missionaries lacks the vital element of a corporate
demonstration of the Christian life in a body of Christian
believers worshipping, living and loving together.

In many Muslim countries, large churches have survived
from the early days when the Christian Church predomin-
ated. The Coptic and Orthodox churches in Lebanon,
Egypt and Jordan stand out as significant examples. Lacking a sweeping biblical reformation, these churches have

often become somewhat stagnant in ritual formalism and may strike the outsider as spiritually and doctrinally deficient. But we cannot ignore the courage and endurance that these Christians have demonstrated in resisting all pressures and clinging to their faith for more than a thousand years of Muslim rule. Signs of biblical and spiritual renewal spring up hopefully in some parts of the great Egyptian Coptic Orthodox Church, but generally Protestant evangelical missionaries will not find it easy to relate to these ancient churches. Nevertheless we have to ask ourselves whether mission to Muslims in these countries should not come through the existing Christian churches there. Over the centuries they may have lost their vision for evangelism among Muslims and concentrated solely on survival, but the Holy Spirit is able to renew their vision and it is possible that the Spirit could even use expatriate personnel as his agents.

Western Christian workers often exhibit an unholy impatience which demands quick results. Many lose hope of ever making any impact on the Christian churches in the country where they are called to work and so they begin Muslim evangelism on their own apart from the national Christians. This trend may be exacerbated by narrow denominationalism or by inability to work with people who differ doctrinally from ourselves. As Christian workers in other lands we need to ask ourselves very carefully and with a minimum of traditional prejudices what churches we can work with and what Christians we can share with in fellowship.

There are times when the expatriate Christian worker may need to give local churches an example in pioneer evangelism among Muslims. Sometimes we can best teach cross-cultural mission by venturing into such work ourselves without waiting for the local churches to catch the vision. So in Britain various movements and missions are working directly among Muslim tourists and immigrants without specific church involvement.

In other situations we may be wiser to work patiently in the fellowship of the national Church, teaching and encouraging them until their churches become such loving fellowships that Muslims are attracted to them and thus to Jesus Christ. Such living examples of the body of Christ will also act as launching pads from which outgoing evangelism may proceed.

Paul went to the relatively open Gentiles in order that the Jews might be provoked to jealousy, longing to enter into the same blessings which the Gentile Christians so manifestly enjoyed. Is this a pattern for us in our desire to share the riches of Jesus Christ with Muslims? Should we seek to work in and through other peoples in order to bring the Gospel to Muslims? If we decide that this is God's purpose for us in our situation, we must be careful that our motives are clear. We do not want to run away from the tough task of Muslim evangelism, escaping into easier forms of mission. We must never lose sight of our calling or of our evangelistic witness to Muslims. Working through existing churches and working directly among Muslims are not mutually exclusive approaches.

4 Groups or individuals?

We have already noted the extreme difficulties encountered by any Muslim who leaves Islam and becomes a Christian. A Christian man in Afghanistan told me how his wife had been taken away from him by her family because they did not wish her to live any more with an apostate. Another young man from a Middle East country told how he would never be able to find a wife, a job or even a place to live. Older people may fear that no one will take responsibility for their burial, for there may not be a local

Christian cemetery while the Muslim burial place would not accept them.

We must seriously question whether it is really possible for one individual on his own to become an open Christian in a staunchly Muslim society. Should we not be aiming rather at the conversion of whole groups? Could we not discuss the Christian faith with whole extended families, with groups of people who work together, with village elders as a group or with other cohesive groupings of people? If they turn to Jesus Christ as a group, it will be much easier for them to exist as Christians in the midst of a hostile society.

At one stage in South Thailand about a dozen Muslim leaders were meeting together regularly to read and discuss a New Testament which had come into their possession. They were so impressed by it that they seriously debated the possibility of turning their respective mosques into churches. If this had happened, one wonders how the local population would have reacted. Would these men have been murdered? Or would they have sparked off a large-scale turning to Christ? Sadly, we do not know the answer, because they finally decided against faith in Christ and their meetings for discussion of the New Testament fizzled out.

In South Thailand I was invited to visit a remote village to have lunch with the headman who came regularly to our mission hospital and had thus become friendly with us. His village stagnated in a remote area at the end of a rough track. Local maps did not condescend to survey the locality. It was a long bicycle ride in the tropical heat, but on my arrival the headman gathered the whole village to hear the message of Jesus Christ and discuss it together. My friend, the headman, presided like a patriarch. All the people of the village were relations of his. Unfortunately I had no missionary training or experience at that stage and I did not see the potential of this village. To me it was just a small remote village of no great importance, one of multitudes of similar places in our area which remained largely un-evangelised. It did not occur to me that the whole community might turn as a group to Christ and thus form a Christian base. In such a Christian community people might develop steadily as Christians without excessive persecution or pressure and then the Gospel could spread out from it into other villages in the whole area. I deeply regret today that I never went back to that village and, as far as I know, no other Christian has visited them again. I believe that I should have given that village priority in the use of my time. It is possible that after more teaching they would have rejected the Gospel of Christ, but it is equally possible that the preaching and teaching would have borne fruit. We cannot prejudge the outcome of our evangelism, for God alone by his Spirit has sovereign control.

Only when we moved from South Thailand to work in the singularly ripe mission field in Indonesia did we realise the significance of group turnings to Christ. Our area was largely animistic, but also included some Muslims. Most of Indonesia is, however, Muslim. Our experiences in North Sumatra can be paralleled in other more solidly Muslim areas. Before we joined the national Church in our part of North Sumatra, they had experienced the joy of seeing a whole battalion of the army turning as a group to Christ. We ourselves witnessed a hospital ward of fifteen men making a group decision to accept Jesus Christ and follow him. What a joy also to see whole families turning to Christ! After we left Indonesia a senior school of some five hundred teenagers responded to the message and they were baptised into the faith of Jesus Christ.

People often ask me how one witnesses when aiming for such a group turning. Let me describe what happened in the hospital. I visited the T.B. ward, preached to the fifteen patients, discussed with them as a group, and sold and distributed Christian literature. Before leaving I suggested to them that they read the books and discuss together the possibility of all becoming Christians. In hospital visiting in England we tend to be very individualistic, witnessing almost in a whisper to one patient and then another. If therefore we see conversions, it will only be one person at a time. In Sumatra we aimed at groups of people.

I have written elsewhere about the theory of group conversions (in *Can My Church Grow?*) and the whole missionary movement owes much in this matter to the Church Growth movement founded by Dr. McGavran of Pasadena, California. We cannot ignore the vital import-ance of this approach for Muslim evangelism. In Britain too we would surely be wise in witness among Muslim immig-rants to pray and work for whole families to be converted.

5 Parabolic preaching

(a) Clear or parabolic?
In the New Testament we are faced with two differing approaches to preaching. In the Book of Acts the apostles concentrated on a definite form of preaching which made the message of Jesus Christ quite specific and clear in his let-ters too the apostle Paul asks for prayer that he may be able to make the Gospel clear as he "ought to speak" (Col. 4:4). On the other hand Jesus himself often used parables in order that his hearers might not understand unless they were spiritually prepared for the message he presented. Mark comments therefore that Jesus did not speak to the people without using parables, but "privately to his own disciples he explained everything" (Mark 4:34).

It would seem that in God's sight mankind may be divided into two groups: those whom God has chosen to be his people and whose eyes are therefore open to his truth form the one group, while the rest of mankind fall into the second category of those who are outside the kingdom of God. Jesus declares that to his elect disciples "has been given the secret of the kingdom of God", but "for those outside everything is in parables" (Mark 4:11).

What does this mean for our witness today? Perhaps we may deduce that we should declare the glories of the Christian message in clear and definite terms to those who are open to the work of the Spirit and are hungry for spiritual life. But for those who are spiritually resistant we should speak in parables.

We all know that it is a sadly hardening experience to hear the Gospel and reject it. The more a man rejects Christ, the harder his heart becomes. With people who are resistant to the Gospel we may therefore be kinder if we do not force them to a decision about Christ before the Holy Spirit has prepared them to receive the Gospel. If we preach in parables, those with spiritually open hearts will discern the significance of our stories. Those with hard hearts will not penetrate below the surface facts of our stories. Let me give an example of a story I have used often among Muslims.

There were once two Muslim men who went to the mosque to pray. The first man was a devout Muslim who had been to Mecca on pilgrimage, prayed regularly five times a day and was known in the community for his piety. He went to the mosque that day with total confidence, for he knew all the prescribed rituals of how to wash himself before entering the mosque, as well as the set movements and words of the prayers. He entered the mosque, went straight to a prominent place in the centre towards the front and performed his prayers with absolute perfection. But while praying his thoughts wandered away to the pretty girl who lived next door and he pictured to himself her shapely figure.

The second man to come to the mosque had lived a

thoroughly rotten life of moral degradation. Having not prayed for many years, he had forgotten the details of the outward rituals of washings, prayer movements and even the words one recited in prayer. But he was deeply aware of the evil of his behaviour and longed to get right with God again, start a new life and make amends for all he had done until then. Shyly he approached the mosque, dipped his hands in the pool of water to wash his hands and face, left his sandals outside the mosque and slipped quietly in. Feeling a bit out of place he went behind a pillar in the hope that no one would see him. Deeply moved with a spirit of repentance he abandoned any attempt to remember the set words and movements of prayers; so he turned to God with simple words of his own.

With which man's prayers was God pleased? Those of us who know the original biblical version of the story may think the answer is obvious, but in Muslim communities without Christian or even Western influence I have usually been given the wrong answer. To many it is obvious that God would be pleased with the man who was obedient to the revealed and prescribed patterns of prayer, although it may be slightly regrettable that his mind yielded to sexual fantasies. On the other hand God could not be pleased with the second man's prayers. His life had not yet had time to do good works to make amends for his past sins. And his prayers were not according to the will of God in the words and movements laid down for Muslims.

In telling this story I have found that worldly Muslims just accept the story at its face value, enjoying lustful speculation about the girl who lived next door and spiteful comments about leading Muslim men in the town. One or two more enlightened people detect that the story contains greater significance. Is God pleased only with external forms or does he look at the heart? How can we get our hearts and motives clean before God? How can we so love

God that we can truly concentrate on him in our praying?

Such seriously enquiring minds may come back to the story-teller later and ask more about the way of life. That is our opportunity to share the deeper truths of the Gospel. It will then come in answer to their requests, not forced upon them by our unsolicited preaching. It will also be in the context of a new understanding that religion is a matter of the heart and not just external forms, for sin is more than failing to perform right rituals.

In many cultures story-telling is a respected art and it is helpful for the Christian witness to gain a reputation as a good story-teller. Obviously I have told the above story without frills in this book, but in reality I like to take much time over a story, embroider it with considerable detail and encourage a maximum of humorous banter. But the discerning see through the light-hearted entertainment to the heart of the matter.

(b) Pictorial or abstract?

Parabolic preaching is not merely a question of whether we want to make our Gospel clear. It also fits because many cultures prefer to think pictorially rather than in abstract philosophical or theological concepts. In former times it used to be said that for doctrinal questions we should examine the Epistles and not the Gospels or Acts. Doctrinal truth, it was said, is not to be proved or formulated through historical writings. More recently scholars have demonstrated how the Gospel writers did actually have a definite didactic purpose in their selection of historical materials. The old argument also ignored the possibility of teaching truth through stories and pictorial language. The Gospels of course give us a marvellous example of how Jesus taught, using vivid pictures from current daily life.

In many cultures today we need to move away from teaching only through abstract concepts and begin to use vivid stories as a didactic means. The story should not be just an illustration which is subordinate to the actual point. The story is in itself the teaching.

(c) Logical or tangential?

As Europeans we have been taught to develop an argument in a logical manner, in which one point leads to another and relates to it in a neat sequence. In discussions with Muslims who have not been unduly influenced by Western educational patterns we may find that this does not work. We may be distressed to find that the Muslim suddenly flies off on a tangent in his thinking, switching the conversation to something quite unrelated to what we were trying to prove. Some word or idea in what we were saying gives rise in his mind to a totally different thought and subject. The two different thoughts may be connected by some expression like "that reminds me that . . ." or "your use of that word makes me think of . . ." Thus, for example, the European may argue logically that since A + B = C, therefore 2 (A+B) = 2C, or B = C–A. But others might develop a different line of logic, e.g. A + B = C; I went for a walk in the moonlight; black is a nice colour, but not for clothes; my wife has a new blue dress; owing to inflation life is expensive; inflation leads to unemployment. The key to this latter chain of logic is that the shape of the letter C reminds us of a moon and it is therefore logical to proceed from the mathematical formula to the thought about a moonlight walk. A walk in the moonlight reminds us of darkness and so of the colour black. The sequence of thought is totally logical and natural, but may frustrate anyone wishing to tell more fully about the formula A + B = C.

Many Western missionaries battle with this problem also within the Church, for they try to teach people of different cultures to preach in our way. We attempt to confine them to neat, systematic preaching whereby every sermon has an introduction, some logically interconnected points and then a clear summary which brings the entire message together into a compact whole. We find it difficult to appreciate a sermon which contains a string of apparently unrelated points, particularly too if stories form the greater part of the talk.

Conclusion

In mission among Muslims we will need to adjust to different principles of communication, whether as a missionary in another country, as a pastor in a church, or as an individual seeking meaningful contact with a Muslim neighbour or colleague. Once these different principles have been understood and grasped, the way forward is clearer and filled with greater hope.

7
The Muslim Convert

In this chapter we face two pressing questions confronting us in mission among Muslims. Firstly we ask whether a believer in Jesus Christ as Lord and Saviour needs to leave the fold of Islam. Can he with a clear conscience remain within the monotheistic faith and practices of Islam but with the addition of Christian doctrine? Secondly we must look at the form of any Christian church which emerges from within a Muslim context; how much of the Muslim background can be carried over into a Christian church?

These two questions depend on our answer to a fundamental theological question concerning our attitude to other faiths. If we believe that Islam is totally demonic, then clearly a convert must make a clean break from everything in his Muslim background. If, on the other hand, we consider Islam to be parallel to Old Testament Judaism, a revelation from God which is inadequate but which is fulfilled and completed in Christ, then we shall encourage the Christian convert to remain rooted in his Muslim background. I doubt whether either of these extreme positions mirrors a truly biblical approach.

Traditional Christian theology has maintained a balance: it holds firm to the idea of the sinful depravity of man and at the same time the fact that something of God's creational image in man remains even after the Fall. In the nature of man therefore the image and likeness of God continues to struggle against the attacks of Satan. But the pervasive infiltration of sin contaminates every part of our lives, so that we talk in terms of the "total" depravity of man. This realistic theology prevents a naive or simplistic misunderstanding of man. We will find vestiges of God's image even in the worst of people (e.g. loyalty to friends, love of children or of a wife), but even these apparently good characteristics are shot through with sin (e.g. human love is always contaminated by pride or selfishness and is never perfect). This basic Christian teaching applies also to our understanding of other faiths. They contain elements of truth and beauty (e.g. Islam's faith in the one Creator God) which Christians rejoice to acknowledge and which form bridges for the fuller truth of the Gospel. But these good aspects are sadly spoiled by demonic untruth (e.g. false views of the character of Allah, as we have noted in previous chapters). Some Christians are therefore asking the wrong question when they query whether Allah is indeed God or whether he is an idol. The answer lies between these two extremes. Allah is God, but the Muslim understanding of his nature needs both addition and correction – as is also true of nominal Christians' use of the name "God" in Britain.

In this chapter we shall therefore assume that the convert from Islam will certainly retain some good elements from his cultural and religious heritage, while renouncing all that stems from Satan and sin.

1 Remain in Islam?

In some strongly Muslim countries conversion from Islam into another faith is tantamount to suicide. Those who come to faith in Jesus Christ must therefore make a radical decision. They can make an open confession of Jesus as Lord and Saviour, be baptised and then probably die the death of a martyr. Otherwise they may perhaps be able to flee the country, find anonymity in Europe or North America and there develop a true Christian life. But they then lose all contact with their own people and have no testimony to them. This second alternative is generally only open to wealthier and more educated men. Many ordinary people eschew the first alternative and cannot afford the second. They opt for a third possibility, namely to continue the outward forms of Islam while adding in their hearts a new spiritual dimension based on the person and work of Jesus Christ. Many of these will in practice live as secret believers.

Some Christian workers would positively discourage believers from cutting themselves off from their Muslim environment by being baptised and professing their faith publicly. The goal of such workers is that eventually sufficient secret believers would be in that society to make it possible to form a church and actually exist as a Christian entity in that Muslim area.

This approach of encouraging converts to remain within the fold of Islam may be theologically undergirded by assuming that Islam stands in a parallel position to pre-Christian Judaism. As Jesus and the apostles continued to worship in the Temple and in the Jewish synagogues, so the Muslim convert may remain within Islam and worship at the mosque. Many of us would however want to query whether Islam can indeed be equated with the Jewish faith, for the Christian accepts totally the revelation of the Old Testament but may be less ready to acknowledge that Mohammed was a prophet of God or that the Quran contains God's revealed word. Is it then possible to give lip-service to the creed of Islam when the faith of Jesus Christ rules in one's heart and mind? The crunch may well come in connection with the regular daily prayer ritual or with some of the great Muslim festivals. The prayers clearly affirm Mohammed as the messenger or prophet of God, which may sour the Christian's conscience. Some of the

festivals are based on the annual pilgrimage to Mecca with
its particular background and theological implications.
Some aspects may be celebrated with an eye to their
fulfilment in Christ (e.g. the animal sacrifice which forms
part of the pilgrimage ritual), but many Christians would
not feel happy to endorse all that the pilgrimage stands for
in Islam.

The question of secret believers who remain within Islam
also raises the hot issue of the nature of the Church. As
Christians we would probably all agree that new birth not
only involves conversion to God in Christ by the Spirit, but
also incorporates us into the Church which is the body of
Christ. Baptism is inseparably connected with conversion
in the Bible, for it is the outward sign of God's covenant
promises to the believer. Conversion to Christ, baptism
and entry into God's Church go hand in hand. What then is
the position of the new believer who remains within Islam
without being baptised? And in the festivals associated with
the pilgrimage he reaffirms that he belongs to the community of Islam; can this be squared with his membership of the
body of Christ, the Church?

It is true that some Christians have emphasised the
spiritual nature of the invisible Church which consists of
true born again believers only. To them the visible Church
may seem an almost unnecessary phenomenon which can
be detrimental to the true faith of Christ and which is
certainly quite secondary to the mystical reality of the
invisible Church. Such Christians see no great problem in
encouraging believers to remain within the outward forms
of Islam while joining their fellow believers in heart and
spirit. But the theological problem is more acute for those
of us who consider it biblically untenable to separate the
invisible reality from its outward and visible manifestation.
To us the internal affairs of the heart must always be
demonstrated in the externals of our faith. We may there-

fore find it hard to accept the possibility of the heart belonging to Christ while the body remains in Islam.

2 Messianic Mosques?

In various Muslim communities today small groups of new Christians are emerging. We are bound to ask therefore what form of Christian church they should develop. And if there is already a church in their area, should they join that church even if it is culturally alien to their Muslim background?

Once again we are forced to face a basic theological question. What does the Bible teach about the Church? As I have written elsewhere, Calvin and his followers tended to assume that the Bible gives us a blueprint for the structures and worship of the Church. We have the responsibility to search the Scriptures, find the biblical pattern and follow it. In that case there should be uniformity among churches in different countries and it makes no difference whether one comes from a Muslim or any other background. The Anglican position, however, has rather affirmed that the Bible does not give clear definitions concerning such matters, but that true churches should have an order which is consonant with the teaching of Scripture. And a few Christians today merely state that the Bible is so unclear that it leaves such peripheral matters to our own discretion.

The weight of scholarship today would seem to lean away from any idea of a biblical blueprint towards the indisputable fact that the early Church based its forms on the religious background from which it sprang. Jewish synagogue worship and structures form the foundation on which the Christian Church was built. It may therefore be claimed that it is biblical for a church to relate closely to the religious and cultural context in which it is placed, although this must never be an excuse for doctrinal or spiritual compromise. This principle has profound implications for the Church in every land, for it means that traditionalism must constantly yield to the pressures of our fast changing cultures. In Islamic societies too the Church will want to adjust to its milieu.

Recently I had the joy of leading some seminars for missionaries in South Thailand working among Malays in that area. A small church has begun to emerge among the otherwise solidly Muslim population. What sort of church should be formed? We needed to ask many questions. What are the patterns of leadership in local Malay society? What is the role of the Muslim *imam*, or priest? How does he relate to the mosque committee and what are the functions or responsibilities of that committee? Only when we had begun to examine that type of question could we think seriously concerning the organisational structures of the church which we trust will grow and flourish in that area in the coming days. We do not want the church to be a foreign import which does not relate culturally to the local people. Roland Allen in his old classic *Missionary Methods – St. Paul's or Ours?* called the Church in China "an exotic". We want to learn from history and the mistakes of the past, so that the Church in Muslim societies may not be culturally offensive.

During those days in South Thailand we also enjoyed seminars together with those missionaries working among Thai Buddhists and again we faced the same sort of questions. In the light of the role of Buddhist monks and abbots, what should be the function of the Christian leaders in a church? With the Buddhist practice that every young man has a short period as a monk in the temple, should we institute something similar in a Christian church?

With reference to the work among both Buddhists and Muslims we turned our attention to issues of worship. The high point of Muslim prayer is the act of prostration in which the Muslim kneels before God with his forehead bowed to the ground. In the Bible too we have accounts of men who demonstrated their worship and awe at the presence of God in similar fashion. Should Christian prayer in a Muslim society practise such agreed ritual movements of the body? Some European Christians may recoil from the word "ritual" because of its associations in their church history, but of course they will not want to impose their particular backgrounds onto Muslim converts in another land. We have to ask rather whether it is biblically allowable and whether it is spiritually helpful.

The Church in a Muslim context must ask whether it is helpful for prayer to be made in the symbolic direction of Jerusalem. Muslims pray towards Mecca; Daniel directed his prayers with his face set towards Jerusalem; should the Muslim convert follow the example of Daniel?

Muslims pray regularly five times a day at the set times of prayer, to which they are summoned by the call to prayer. This call is always made by human voice, and never with the use of musical instruments or bells. Ought the emerging Christian church to do likewise? In some sections of the Christian Church the hours of the day are punctuated by the seven worship offices, so such a regular round of prayer times is not unknown in the Christian tradition. And certainly there is no need to export the use of church bells, which may easily be exchanged for a human voice calling believers to worship and prayer.

Muslim prayer commences with ritual washing, for no believer would feel happy to enter the presence of God unwashed. As Christians we know that God looks at the heart rather than the outward body, desiring pure motives and not just clean hands. But the ritual washing of the body before prayer can symbolise the deeper cleansing of the heart. Perhaps we may fairly say that the Muslim rituals parallel the traditional Christian's use of a Sunday suit and the wearing of smart clothes to church. In every tradition the Church must battle with the insidious danger of mere externalism.

Should the actual building of the church be more akin to a mosque? Are the usual European fashions a necessity? Do we need seats in a church? Must the focal point be a table or a pulpit? Do we need a special lectern?

And then comes the question of the fast month. In connection with prayer, fasting is encouraged in the New Testament. Jesus gives teaching on the snare of pride in fasting and the dangers of sanctimonious piety, but true fasting has a significant place in Christian devotion. Is it permissible to introduce a fast month along Muslim lines into a Christian church? Of course it must be voluntary and practised in conjunction with prayer. Good teaching from the New Testament would then instruct believers in the basic principles of Christian fasting.

Some new converts from Islam rebel against everything to do with their old form of religion and may prefer to make a clean break, renouncing even the cultural forms of Islam. After an initial period, however, they may develop sufficient spiritual maturity to enjoy having their Christian faith dressed in Islamic cultural garb. And many other Muslims may find it easier to become Christians if this does not involve a total break with all that they have loved in their upbringing. We do not want people to be discouraged from Christian discipleship by the church's alien nature.

In many countries today the Church is associated with very different racial, religious and cultural backgrounds from the Muslim population. In Pakistan, for example, the Church uses vocabulary which originates in a Hindu background and which to the Muslim therefore smacks of idolatry and polytheism. In Egypt and Lebanon the Christian and Muslim communities have lived for centuries in considerable isolation from each other. They have developed different lifestyles and cultures, so that conversion is not just a religious transformation; it also involves a change from one community to the other. In Sudan the Church is associated with the African tribal groups from the south, whereas the Muslims in the north follow Islam.

Today in several situations Muslim converts are beginning to form new Christian groupings with an Islamic cultural form. At present such groups are very much in their infancy, but they may represent a significant trend for the future of Muslim evangelism. In many ways this movement follows in the footsteps of Jewish Christians, some of whom have determined not to lose their Jewish identity and merge into Gentile churches. They have therefore formed "Messianic synagogues".

Over the past few years there has been considerable debate in mission thinking about the rightness of such fellowships or churches which are for one race, class or cultural grouping. They face real dangers of exclusivism and therefore of racial or class pride. They can also easily fail to learn from churches of other cultural backgrounds, as has been so very evident in many middle-class white European churches. Just as they can easily deny the New Testament teaching on the loving unity of Christ which breaks down all barriers of race, class and sex, so too they often lose sight of God's call to his people to evangelise all nations. On the other hand a one-culture fellowship attracts non-Christians of that culture more easily and its worship and teaching are well suited to the people present. This is not the place for a longer or fuller discussion of this whole question of the so-called 'homogeneous unit principle', but this may well prove a vital issue for the whole future of Christian witness among Muslims.

Conclusion

In coming years we may see new Christian churches which
are outwardly as closely akin to Muslim mosques as the
early Christians were to their Jewish synagogue background.

8
The Church Today in Muslim Societies

In the last chapter we discussed the sort of Church which could come into existence through pioneer evangelism in Muslim areas. It is always a delight to think through similar questions with regard to our own country. If there had been no previous Christian history and we could plant a totally new Church in our country, what forms of church structures or worship would we encourage? But actually the Church does already exist in most situations and we have to take into account the historical traditions and patterns which have evolved over the years. Nevertheless it may be helpful to pray through such questions so that we do not passively accept the norms of a past culture in our church life, but have clear goals and aims as we seek to steer the Church into the future.

In many Muslim lands also the Church exists already and in this chapter we want to look at the representatives of Christ who are his ambassadors in such lands. In previous chapters we have several times noted the difficulty of mission among Muslims and the danger that we may lose heart and turn back from the task to which our Lord has called us. It may prove good for us therefore to see how God has marvellously planted his Church in many Muslim societies. Although in most cases we cannot record sensational growth in the Christian Church in such areas, yet it is encouraging to see that Islam is not totally impregnable against the witness of the Christian Gospel. Our hope is built not only on the confidence of faith that God will in the future work amongst Muslims, but also on the already observable fact that God has worked and is working now in bringing Muslims to faith in Jesus Christ as Lord and Saviour. It is not possible in this chapter to look at the opportunities for mission among Muslims in every country, but I shall select a few typical or significant areas.

1 Indonesia

Indonesia shines as the great exception in Muslim evangelism, for many thousands become Christians every year and the Church grows rapidly. The islands of Indonesia stretch for some 3,000 miles from west of the Malaysian peninsula almost across to Australia. Population statistics rapidly become outdated, for the current figure of approximately 150 million breeds an additional 4–4½ million every year. A high proportion of Indonesians huddle together on the grossly over-populated island of Java, while the huge outer islands of Sumatra and the Celebes and multitudes of other smaller islands shelter relatively sparse populations. The government naturally attempts to encourage people to move from Java to cultivate the land on other islands. Many of these migrant Javanese people have proved very open to the Christian message and large numbers of churches have been established among them.

The Indonesian Christian Church has a long history behind it. By the seventeenth century the Reformed churches of Holland were already vying with the Roman Catholic successors of Francis Xavier for spiritual supremacy. The early converts came largely from those racial groups which had not yet entered the community of Islam, but still clung to their traditional tribal religions. But the Church grew. As Stephen Neill has pointed out in *A History of Christian Missions* the Dutch claimed 100,000 Christians in

Java and 40,000 in Ambon by the end of the seventeenth century. In spite of the fact that the New Testament was translated into the local language (Malay) by 1688, yet the standard of biblical teaching and spiritual life left much to be desired. Nevertheless God continued to build his Church and over the following centuries it became one of the largest Churches in the world.

My wife and I went to work in North Sumatra in 1961 and Christians were rejoicing in the growth of the Church. Whereas there had been only about 1½ million indigenous Protestant Christians in the mid 1930s and about 3¼ million by 1956, in the early 1960s the Church had grown to approximately 5 million. This steady growth gave a good foundation for the unusual spiritual openness which followed the attempted coup d'état by the Communists in 1965. In the following two or three years the Church mushroomed by several millions before settling down again to an estimated annual growth of about 7 per cent. By 1980, however, the Church probably numbered some 25–30 million members, so even a mere annual growth of 7 per cent represents very considerable numbers.

The missionary potential of such a huge Church cannot be overestimated. When one considers the significant impact on world mission made by such relatively small churches as the Dutch, British or German, then one realises the enormous possibilities if the Indonesian Church caught a vision for worldwide mission. This potential is further increased by the fact that large numbers of the Indonesian Christians come from Muslim backgrounds.

But sadly we observe little evidence of active worldwide mission by the majority of Indonesian churches. The blame lies partly at the door of the Western missionaries who have often failed to teach the Indonesian Church its responsibility to other nations and peoples. It should also be said that the harvest is so great and so ripe in Indonesia itself that the churches have their hands full within their own country. But that is not an adequate excuse, for the same could have been said of the Jewish apostles in the early years of Christian history. If the apostles had waited until Israel was adequately evangelised before beginning with wider Gentile mission, they would certainly not have brought the Gospel to the heathen peoples of Europe.

Perhaps the main reason for the failure of the Indonesian churches to play a full role in world mission is their lack of adequate teaching and leadership. Thus Latourette says in his *Christianity in a Revolutionary Age* that "a major problem of Indonesian Protestantism was the recruiting and training of an indigenous clergy". Already in the early years of the Indonesian Church trained leadership was sadly lacking. Thus in 1776 there were only five ordained ministers in all Indonesia who spoke the Malay language. And still in more recent years the training of Christian leadership has lagged sadly behind the numerical growth of the Church. In our area of North Sumatra the average minister had overall responsibility for some twelve congregations.

In some ways, therefore, the Christian observer grieves at the unfulfilled missionary potential of the Indonesian Churches. On the other hand we can rejoice at the huge number of men and women from Muslim and other religious backgrounds who are finding new life and salvation in Jesus Christ. And we do see the small beginnings of a missionary vision. Already before the Second World War the Batak churches of North Sumatra had sent missionaries to the Dyaks of Sarawak, East Malaysia and to the aboriginal tribes of West Malaysia. In more recent years the wide vision of the Rev. Octavianus and some other leading Christians has challenged Christians to world-wide mission.

Clearly the vital task of Christian missions in Indonesia is to teach and train the existing Christian churches with the aim that they should evangelise their own nation and also play a leading role in world mission. Sadly, many foreign missionaries lack such strategic thinking and are working outside and often even in competition with the national churches of Indonesia.

2 Malaysia

Across the water from Indonesia lies the land of Malaysia, consisting of the West Malaysian peninsula and the East Malaysian Sarawak and Sabah. In the former about 45 per cent of the population is Malay and therefore Muslim, while in East Malaysia traditional tribal religions, Islam and Christianity struggle together for the allegiance of the large tribal populations. The Christian Church has traditionally been active among the Chinese and Indians of West Malaysia, but has made no impact at all on the Muslims. With governmental power in the hands of the Muslim Malays it has been made illegal to evangelise Muslims and there is considerable pressure for people to convert to Islam. Job promotion is often linked to financial inducements to persuade men to follow Islam.

Since the mid 1970s sweeping revival has revitalised the tribal Churches of East Malaysia, stimulating Christians to a new evangelistic passion. It was for me personally a great encouragement to be invited for a Bible-teaching tour in some of these Churches. In some places people walked for three days to attend a meeting, because they were hungry for teaching. In one area I found that the revival had touched the whole population; eventually the Muslim government saw that the police were no longer required there and they were withdrawn. Inevitably in such a movement of the Spirit there have been some excesses and the need for pastoral care and Bible teaching is great, but we rejoice in the transformation of lives and the vigorous Christian witness of the Church. Such vibrant revival life inevitably overflows and affects others.

When travelling to one such revival area in Sarawak I sat next to a New Zealander on the plane. He worked for a large oil company and was clearly a man of the world. But when he heard where I was going his face brightened. He had been on holiday there recently, staying in an official government rest house. On his first morning the servants had woken him very early in the morning to attend the dawn prayer meeting. Hard-bitten and irreligious in background, he had not anticipated an early morning prayer meeting on holiday! But he was given no alternative. He told me how he had been touched by God's Spirit that first morning, although he could not speak the local language and therefore did not understand a word of the prayer meeting.

Most of the evangelistic work of these tribal Churches is directed towards other tribal groups who are still following traditional primal religions. But some Muslims are also being touched by the lively faith of the Christians. Some of the tribal young people migrate to West Malaysia for further education. Because of their official standing as indigenous peoples they can attend the colleges normally reserved for Malays and thus bring a Christian witness into these bastions of Islam. Conversions among Malay Muslim students have been reported.

East Malaysian tribal believers are not the only Christians with a witness among Muslims. Increasing numbers of Chinese Christians both in Malaysia itself and also in the politically and religiously freer atmosphere of Singapore are widening their missionary vision to include their Malay neighbours. As a result one may now find the occasional Malay Christian in largely Chinese or Indian congregations. The signs are that increasing numbers of Malays are becoming disillusioned with the growth of strongly tradi-

tional and militant Islam, so that we may well see more
turning to Christ in the coming years. (In Iran too it is said
that more Muslims have been turning to Christ than in
previous years as a reaction against the rule of Islam under
Khomeini.) Fierce social opposition and even state
persecution has made it almost impossible for a Malay to
stand openly as a Christian, but unobtrusively some find
their way to faith in Christ. This trend is encouraged by the
increasing use of the Malay language by Christians, for the
government has insisted on the unification of the peoples of
Malaysia through Malay as the national language.

3 Tropical Africa

Islam has spread along the coastal strips of East Africa and
down from the north in West Africa. The Christian faith,
on the other hand, has advanced from the coast in West
Africa and has become strong further inland in East Africa.
The constant trend away from traditional tribal faiths in
favour of a major world religion has added urgency to the
missionary task of both faiths.

In the past both Islam and Christianity have concentrated their missionary attention on those tribes which were
still following primal religions, but over the past few years
increasing emphasis has been given in some Christian
circles to witness among Muslims. In Nigeria the churches
were mobilised for active mission through the New Life for
All campaign which stimulated many Christians to share
their faith with Muslim neighbours. As a result some
Muslims turned to Jesus Christ. The impetus of this movement has now largely declined, but it has left a heritage of
interest in the possibility of Muslims being converted and
therefore of encouragement to the Christians. In Ghana,
too, witness among Muslims bears steady fruit. The earlier
danger that Christians did not even consider the possibility
of sharing their faith with Muslims still needs to be coun-

tered, but increasingly Christians have become aware of their responsibility. This interest in evangelism among Muslims is fostered by the interdenominational evangelical Nigerian Islam in Africa Project (N.I.A.P.).

When my wife and I were in Kenya recently, we were much encouraged to find an Anglican minister with a warm vision for Muslim evangelism. He is working hard to share this vision with others, so that they will join with him in evangelism among the many Muslims in the big cities and also towards the coast. We also enjoyed meeting again with some Norwegian former students of ours who are working in Muslim areas of East Africa and are finding that some young people are quite open to the Gospel.

But there are large areas of tropical Africa where Islam holds unrivalled sway and where the Gospel of Jesus Christ has not penetrated at all. Some pioneer missions struggle to gain a toe-hold in these communities, but the task is not an easy one. Those of us in relatively easier mission situations have a responsibility to support such workers in every possible way.

In many of the countries of tropical Africa we are able to work among Muslims in full-time direct evangelism in cooperation with the existing Churches of these countries. In some areas however we may be wiser to send workers in their secular professions as "tent-makers". Direct evangelism is particularly suited to those tribal groups where Islam is still not very firmly established or where some people follow Islam and others are Christian or still animistic. Strongly Muslim areas where Islam has been firmly established over several centuries may require a more patient and gradual approach through medical, educational, agricultural or other professional personnel with a quiet Christian witness.

4 Immigrants and students in Europe

We have already noted the large numbers of Muslims who are migrating to Europe as students, immigrants or as refugees from countries like Iran. While the older generation of such immigrants tend to huddle together in defensive isolation against the threat of the surrounding alien culture, many of the younger people are open to the new way of life and therefore to new ideas and even to new religious beliefs. A steady trickle of young men and women are becoming Christians.

I was recently in Sweden for a lecture tour and spoke one evening in Uppsala on Marxism and Christianity. The talk was translated into Parsi for the benefit of a group of Iranian men, who had fled from the Khomeini regime and taken refuge in Sweden. They knew that the only viable alternative to the present political and religious order seems to be Marxism, but they were not enamoured of the Soviet and East European outworkings of Marxism. Could Marxism produce adequate answers for Iran? Or is there some other alternative philosophy of life? One or two have already come to see the Christian way as an answer to their needs. Others posed searching questions over coffee after the meeting.

This encounter with Iranian students in Sweden reminded me of a visit to a British public school where I had met a young Iranian lad in the Christian Union. He and his sister have both become active Christians and they are praying for the conversion of their parents in Iran. Through young people converted in Europe the Gospel can reach more personally and effectively into other countries. Thus the "Sevener" branch of the Shi'ites forms a close-knit community which cannot be easily penetrated by outsiders. But a young Pakistani Sevener converted in Britain is in contact with her family, who must surely wonder what it is about the Christian faith which has drawn her to leave

Islam and follow Jesus Christ. With the presence of so many Muslims in our midst in Europe, God has granted to us a new opening for Christian mission which can reach to areas of the world which might otherwise be closed to the messengers of Jesus Christ.

The European Christian enjoys many opportunities for showing the love of Christ to Muslims living or studying in our countries. Attacked by homesickness and loneliness the immigrant will respond warmly to the hospitably open home of a Christian. We can help with the study of English or with free tuition in young people's school or college studies. The older generation find grave difficulty in coping with our bureaucracy – we can help them fill up the right forms and deal with the necessary red tape of social welfare. Practical friendliness means much and will break down prejudice. If we can introduce Muslim friends to our fellow Christians in the church, we may also be helping other Christians to gain a loving concern for their immigrant neighbour. And so the ripples of Christ's love spread.

5 Afghanistan

The rape of Afghanistan by the Soviet Union and the consequent cruel fighting brings in its wake untold suffering. Violence and hunger stalk the people of this backward land. Three million refugees have flooded into Pakistan with all the problems that such a deluge of displaced people inevitably causes. Inside Afghanistan the Muslim fighters are locked in battle with the forces of Communism. But what about the Christian Gospel?

I was recently given the opportunity to visit Afghanistan as a tourist and enjoyed visiting some of the splendid historical sites. The awesome ruggedness of the scenery leaves the visitor breathless. But my special joy was to discover that there are lively Christians in the midst of the largely Muslim population. I had assumed that there would not be any Christians in this solidly Muslim land or that they would be infinitesimal in number. It is of course impossible to give any sort of accurate statistics in a situation where indigenous Christians may be savagely persecuted and therefore cannot meet openly. But I gathered that there are now several hundred Christians in various parts of the country and that new believers are being constantly added to their number. It is encouraging to be reminded that the Christian Gospel can survive and even flourish in the most hostile conditions.

6 The Middle East

Optimists affirm that every grey cloud has with it a silver lining. Pessimists may rather stress that the minuscule silver lining is constantly accompanied by a large thick dark cloud. In looking at Christian mission and the Church in the heartlands of Islam the pessimist may rightly emphasise the huge areas where the Gospel of Jesus Christ is quite unknown and total populations in which no indigenous Christian shines as a light for Christ. It is certainly true that in those lands where Islam wiped out the Church a thousand years ago the Christian Church has found it singularly hard to establish a foothold among local people. From Mauretania in the west of North Africa through Algeria, Tunisia, Libya and down into the Arabian peninsula there is little evidence of a Christian presence. Missions have struggled to establish local churches, but they still remain tiny and weak flotsam in the great eddies of Islam all around them. Direct persecution decimates their numbers, while discrimination and other pressures push them into a defensive attitude which lacks vibrant expectation and hope. Only a very few brave and faithful men and women overcome the fearful odds which are stacked against them.

The situation in these countries is made more difficult by the fact that governments do not permit any direct mission work, give no visas to missionaries and often forbid local people to hear the Gospel, let alone to convert to the Christian faith.

But optimists will want to point out the great opportunities which present themselves to us as Christians these days. The door for expatriate Christians to enter these countries is wide open, if they are willing to continue in their professions. Engineers, architects, oil men, medical personnel, businessmen and teachers or lecturers can gain entrance into lands where missionaries are excluded. Although pay will be generous and living conditions plush, problems will abound. They may well be so busy in their jobs that there will be little time for personal contacts and socialising. The government may locate them in homes which are isolated from the local population. Their lack of language study will militate against their making any deep relationships locally. Nevertheless those Christians with vision and determination will search for opportunities to meet people and have a wise and quiet witness.

Expatriate Christians can also have a significant role in encouraging and teaching the multitude of other expatriates from America, Europe, Asia and the Middle East. Large Christian groups and churches exist among these foreign workers, but few have any missionary aim and even fewer have adequate knowledge, either of their own faith or of Islam, to be able to communicate Jesus Christ effectively. The door is wide open to help such people and thus through them to have a witness to the local Muslim population. Expatriates are also doing invaluable work from outside these countries through the ministries of radio, correspondence courses and other literature work.

Silver linings do already exist. In most of these countries there are indeed small Christian groups. Many of these are growing. They form the small seed which will surely grow into a large tree in coming years. We also understand that there are many secret believers who have not yet had the courage to stand out openly as Christians or are not convinced that the time is ripe for such a definite stand. If a greater liberalism towards the Christian faith comes to prevail because of the growth of the Church or because of a more tolerant attitude in society, then we may expect a considerable number of these secret believers to declare their faith more openly.

But perhaps the greatest grounds for optimism lie in the old traditional churches which have survived through centuries of Muslim pressure in Egypt, Lebanon, Jordan, Israel and other countries. We may be tempted to discount them because of the extreme ritualism and the lack of biblical teaching which sometimes militate against any witness to their Muslim neighbours. Over the centuries a strong community sense has developed which separates them from the surrounding Muslim population. Knowing their history and admiring their perseverance in faith, we shall sympathise with their position. But we long for the Holy Spirit to revitalise these churches in accordance with biblical truth, for in them lies the key to Christian mission in North Africa and the Middle East. Christian radio, correspondence courses and other foreign mission activities will certainly help, but surely the ancient indigenous churches must form the foundation upon which Christian mission will be built. How encouraging therefore to hear of little revival flames flickering in the Coptic Orthodox Church of Egypt. We long that those small flames may lick into the whole body of the Church until the fire burns hotly. Such a fire would doubtless spread into surrounding Muslim communities. But as we rejoice in such a vision we are saddened by the tragic news of Christian–Muslim community fighting both in Egypt and in Lebanon. In such an atmosphere it becomes singularly hard for Christians to have any true witness among Muslims.

In the light of the history of the Church in these lands and in view of the realities of the current situation we dare not be light-heartedly naive concerning Christian mission in North Africa and the Middle East, but we do see small signs that give us hope that God is planning to do a new thing. In the expatriate Christian worker in these countries vibrant hope and vision will need to be tempered with patience, perseverance, wisdom and real love.

Conclusion

In considering Christian mission among Muslims the Christian faces unusually severe tests. Intellectually he struggles to relate his faith to the theological and philosophical world of Islam. All our traditional theological beliefs will need to be challenged and rethought. Likewise the Muslim's patterns of thought and speech cause us to formulate the Gospel anew, so that traditional ways of witnessing become quite unacceptable. This of course also means that mere translations of Western Christian literature are very unsatisfactory. Spiritually too the Christian is engaged in very real warfare. In his book on *The Influence of Animism on Islam* Zwemer shows how animistic and spiritistic beliefs and practices pervade Islam. He quotes Gottfried Simon as saying that Islam has "relaid the old animistic foundations of the heathen's religion and run up a light, artistic superstructure upon it of Muslim customs". Likewise Dr. Adriani asserts that "Muslim ritual, instead of bringing a man to God, serves as a drag net for animism." Certainly it is true that the Christian will face considerable spiritual battles when living in an Islamic milieu. This will be compounded by a possible sense of failure and frustration as he sees little fruit for his labours. His precarious situation as a foreigner in a country which is definitely hostile to his faith demands unusual wisdom. He will often be unable to express his love for the Lord in open verbal witness and will sympathise deeply with Jeremiah when he said "If I say 'I will not mention him, or speak any more in his name', there is in my heart as it were a burning fire shut up in my bones, and I am weary with holding it in, and I cannot" (Jer. 20:9).

As we sense our total inadequacy for such a formidable task, we are forced again to return to the Lord. Both in the call of the disciples (Mark 3:14, 15) and in the missionary commission of Matthew 28:18–20 the divine call to mission is accompanied by the assurance of authority and power. In the Book of Acts too the early Christians found that God filled them anew with the Holy Spirit when they faced a new and demanding task. While it is true that without Christ we can do nothing (John 15:5), we have the confidence that in Christ all things become possible (Matt. 19:26; Mark 9:23). We dare not be glib in mouthing the old formula that "when God calls, he enables" but it is the sure basis for our confidence as we face the urgent call to mission among Muslims.